LE CORBUSIER

THE DECORATIVE ART OF TODAY

translated and introduced by
James I. Dunnett

The Architectural Press: London

L'Art décoratif d'aujourd'hui first published in 1925 by Editions Crès, Paris
Reprinted 1959, 1980
This translation first published in 1987 by the
Architectural Press, 9 Queen Anne's Gate, London SW1H 9BY

French text © Fondation Le Corbusier, 1959
Translation, Introduction and Notes © James I. Dunnett, 1987

BRITISH LIBRARY CATALOGUING IN PUBLICATION DATA

Le Corbusier
 The decorative art of today.
 1. Decoration and ornament, Architectural
 Rn: Charles Edouard Jeanneret   II. Title   III. L'Art décoratif
 d'aujourd'hui. *English*
 729   NA3485

 ISBN 0–85139–015–3

Typeset by Phoenix Photosetting, Chatham
Printed and bound by Billings, Worcester

TABLE OF CONTENTS

Publisher's advertisement from Le Corbusier's *Almanach d'architecture moderne* (1927) showing the original covers of the four books collected from *L'Esprit Nouveau*.

INTRODUCTION

The Decorative Art of Today is a paradoxical title for a book by Le Corbusier, as he was well aware. *'Modern decorative art is not decorated'*, he says. Neither, he might have added, is it art: that is the main burden of the book. By 'decorative art' was meant what is now called 'design', in other words the design of objects of use generally, below the scale of architecture. Le Corbusier's book was to appear at the time of the great 1925 Exposition des Arts Décoratifs in Paris, on which it was effectively a commentary, and so he was obliged to use the same name. But the chapter entitled 'The Decorative Art of Today' is pointedly illustrated by 'standard' objects entirely devoid of decoration. The style now popularly associated with that exhibition, known as 'Art Deco', is one of his principal targets.

As a book on 'design' it took its place in the quartet of books based on articles from *L'Esprit Nouveau*, alongside *Vers une architecture* (Towards a New Architecture), *Urbanisme* (The City of Tomorrow), and *La Peinture moderne*. They all followed a similar format and aphoristic style, and together covered the four 'visual arts' fields of architecture, town planning, painting, and design. 'These four volumes', wrote Le Corbusier in 1927, 'comprised the theory of which the Pavilion [of L'Esprit Nouveau at the 1925 exhibition] was intended to be the realisation.'

Urbanisme and *Vers une architecture* were of course translated into English soon after publication. *L'Art décoratif d'aujourd'hui* has had to wait for the centenary of Le Corbusier's birth, although arguably it provides a more cogent exposition of his general theory of design than either. At a time when his supposed influence is disparaged as never before, it is hoped that this translation will allow his thought to be more fully understood. The changed climate of opinion over the last twenty years has indeed made it now possible to read *Decorative Art* with almost the same reaction as when it first appeared in 1925. Then, according to Maximilien Gauthier in his authorised biography of 1943, *Le Corbusier, ou l'Architecture au service de l'homme*, its publication caused the greatest shock of all Le Corbusier's books. It is certainly an attacking book to a greater extent than its companions, and in our conservation-conscious times its rejection of virtually the whole history of decorative ornament may seem provocative and even offensive in a way that it would not have done twenty years ago. Its iconoclasm was deliberate: 'Since iconolatry [i.e. indulgence in ornament] thrives as virulently as a cancer, let us be iconoclasts.' But its purpose was serious. Le Corbusier had a confidence that few feel now that the 'machine age' could find expression in a different but more beautiful world.

The vigour of Le Corbusier's writing remains immensely stimulating, but our perspective on it has inevitably changed; our interest in it as history has grown. Indeed part of the appeal of *Decorative Art* now lies in the vividness with which it evokes the intellectual milieu of Paris in the early 1920s, with its references by name to contemporary and near-contemporary figures. We see Le Corbusier grappling with the beginnings of Surrealism ('the production of the machine age is a *realist* object capable of high poetry' [my italics]), presenting his version of the recent history of design, constructing a Purist still-life out of standard glassware (c.f. the illustrations on pages 94 and 97), and perhaps making a sly reference to Marcel Duchamp's *Urinal* in his choice of a bidet 'Maison Pirsoul' as the introductory illustration for the chapter devoted to museums. *Decorative Art* has a personal and topical touch, and it was perhaps this which once caused Reyner Banham, more than twenty years ago, to dismiss it as 'a polemical work of only local interest'. The indications are that Le Corbusier did not think so; the issues it raises are so fundamental and its documentary value has become so great that it can now be seen to be a work of major importance.

The purpose of this translation is therefore simply to make the text available in English, with the minimum of commentary, and let it speak for itself – as do Frederick Etchells' excellent translations of its companion volumes. But a very brief indication of the intellectual background may be useful.

The immediate sources of Le Corbusier's argument are very clear – the writings of Adolf Loos and the debate within the Deutscher Werkbund between Henry Van de Velde and Hermann Muthesius and their followers. Loos' essays may first have come to Le Corbusier's notice when a selection was printed in the magazine *Der Sturm* in 1912, and he himself reprinted the most famous, 'Ornament and Crime' written in 1908, in the first issue of *L'Esprit Nouveau* (1920). His absolute rejection of ornament must owe much to the influence of this 'sensational article', and he credits Loos a little grudgingly with the formulation: *the more cultivated a people becomes, the more decoration disappears*. His primary argument asserting the importance of the distinction between a work of art and an object of use can also be found in Loos. Indeed some passages in *Decorative Art* are directly reminiscent of him.

Loos wrote in his essay 'Men's Fashion', reprinted in the collection *Ins Leehre Gesprochen* published in Paris in 1921: 'But the English mock the German's craving for beauty. The Medici Venus, the Pantheon, a picture by Botticelli, a song by Burns – of course these are beautiful. But trousers? Or whether a jacket has three or four buttons?' This seems to find an echo in Le Corbusier's 'first of all the Sistine Chapel, afterwards chairs and filing cabinets: without doubt this is a question of the secondary level, just as the cut of a man's jacket is of secondary importance in his life'.

Le Corbusier was also very familiar with the debates about design in Germany before the First World War, as a result of his travels and research there in 1910–11 on a grant from the municipality of La Chaux-de-Fonds (his native town). His use of the word 'type' as in 'type-needs' and 'type-furniture' clearly owes much to the advocacy by Muthesius, Bruno Paul and others of *Typisierung* and *Typenmöbel*, and carried most of the same connotations. 'Standardization' is not an adequate translation, with its predominant sense of a mechanically reproduced uniformity; what was envisaged was rather the dignified and modest consistency exemplified by many folk or vernacular products, an 'archetypal' solution which attracted no more attention to utilitarian objects than their role demanded. Van de Velde can be understood as the unspoken target of many of Le Corbusier's attacks directed at the Arts and Crafts movement in general and its belief, in the words of William Morris, that 'The true secret of happiness lies in taking a genuine interest in all the details of daily life, in elevating them by art, instead of handing them over to unregarded drudges.'

Political thought at the time may also have played a part. Decoration had been discredited not only by the over-indulgence permitted by mechanical methods of production and the attacks on this 'fraud' by the Arts and Crafts movement, but also by attacks such as those of the sociologist Thorstein Veblen, who stigmatised it in his influential book *The Theory of the Leisure Class* (1899) as 'conspicuous consumption'. He wrote: "This process of selective adaptation of designs to the end of conspicuous waste, and the substitution of pecuniary [i.e. ornamental] beauty for aesthetic beauty, has been especially effective in the development of architecture. It would be difficult to find a modern civilized residence or public building which can claim anything better than relative inoffensiveness in the eyes of anyone who will dissociate the elements of beauty from those of honorific waste. . . Considered as objects of beauty the dead walls of the back and sides of these structures left untouched by the hands of the artist are commonly the best feature of the building.' This theme is perhaps reflected by Le Corbusier when he refers to decoration as simply 'promoting decorum'.

But to the ideas of that generation he added two important ingredients: an enthusiasm for the machine itself, seen as the epitome of intellectual mastery – an enthusiasm made possible by the supersession of the Futurists – and a continuous passionate emphasis on the importance of the work of art, which inspires many of the most moving passages in this book. Unlike his mentors, Le Corbusier was able to envisage a new language of art to match his theory, a language considerably inspired by the discoveries of the Cubist painters around 1910 – a language of pure plane, volume, and space, as expressive as any that relied on applied ornament. This combination produced the potent mixture of Le Corbusier's 'propaganda', which has inspired more than one generation. Loos and Muthesius ultimately remained rooted in the craft world of the nineteenth century. They were not able to produce a new image, and their writing seemed essentially negative.

Le Corbusier's strength also lay in the scope of his thought. He was able to develop his doctrine into a theory extending from the scale of the ink-pot to the scale of the city. Both were 'tools' (*outils*) and carried the same obligation: the duty to allow and encourage 'meditation': 'Now and always there is a hierarchy. There is a time for work, when one uses oneself up, and also a time for meditation, when one recovers one's bearing and rediscovers harmony.' 'Meditation' was a synonym for the creation of a work of art, a usage inspired by Cubist paintings, which Le Corbusier saw as essentially meditative. The duty of the 'tool' was to free man for 'meditation' as thus defined: 'Making use of these tools, we avoid unpleasant tasks, accidents, the sterile drudgery . . . and, having won our freedom, we think about something – about art for example (for it is very comforting).'

An ink-pot that was a tool should be modest, functional, and self-effacing (smooth and round, like that of Lenin in Chapter 1), to leave the mind free to concentrate on the affairs of the spirit. A city that was a tool should facilitate culture-giving human contact by the efficiency of its circulation, bring peace of mind by the orderliness of its plan, and provide conditions in the home of calm and light, air and space, conducive to meditation. And so the city is built tall and spacious, open to the sky and set in green parks, intersected by elevated roads planned on an orthogonal grid.* A house that was a tool, or a 'machine for living in', should be whitewashed, for 'There may be some people who think against a background of black. But the tasks of our age – so strenuous, so full of danger, so victorious, seem to demand of us that we think against a background of white.'

As Le Corbusier says in his introduction to the 1959 edition of *Decorative Art*: 'We had undertaken to put up a pavilion of L'Esprit Nouveau which would indissolubly link the equipment of the home (furniture) to architecture (the space inhabited, the dwelling) and to urbanism (the conditions of life of a society).' This book provides the key as perhaps no other does. Essentially, if offers a definition of taste. If the logical extension of its argument that objects of use cannot be works of art would seem to be that they cannot have aesthetic value, that would be a misunderstanding: 'Works of decorative art are tools, *beautiful* tools' says Le Corbusier (my italics), and 'The task of the decorative arts (who will think of a better name?) is above all to make us feel comfortable by serving us politely and helpfully. After that, it is to thrill us, let there be no mistake.' Nevertheless, the problem of 'machines for sitting in, for filing, for lighting, type-machines' remained one

---

*I have discussed this more fully in my article 'The Architecture of Silence', *Architectural Review*, October 1985.

'of purification, of simplication, of precision, before the problem of poetry'.

All this is consistent with Le Corbusier's own venture into furniture design five years later, when he exhibited the famous tubular metal pieces intended for mass-production. They had been designed in collaboration with Charlotte Perriand, who had herself been fired with enthusiasm by *Decorative Art* when it first appeared. But for the Esprit Nouveau pavilion in 1925 – a 'show flat' for the Contemporary City – he had, as a statement of principle, selected only mass-produced items that were already available – Thonet bentwood sidechairs, Maples armchairs, laboratory glassware (all singled out for praise in *Decorative Art*), as well as one or two products of 'folk culture'. These were 'type-objects', whilst on the walls hung major Cubist and Purist paintings – 'provokers of feeling'. A clear division. Later he was to become more ready to accept intermediate categories, just as machine-symbolism was to find a less obvious place in his work and theory. But the underlying thought remained and continued to provide him with an essential discipline.

The Decorative Art of Today is based on a collection of articles from a magazine (mostly published in 1924), and the sequence of thought from chapter to chapter (and sometimes within a chapter) is not always easy to follow. But its import is finally clear enough, and is reinforced by Le Corbusier's vivid choice of illustrations. In this translation I have attempted to retain as much of the distinctive rhythms of Le Corbusier's style as possible – for example, the long strings of nouns in apposition – even when these may not be entirely consistent with a smooth English style. The original page layouts have also been followed. Certain French words always present a problem of translation – for example, *système* and *esprit* – and when these come together in a key definition of architecture '*L'Architecture est un système de l'esprit qui fixe dans un mode matériel le sentiment resultant d'une époque*', the problem becomes a crux, one which has to be seen in the context of Le Corbusier's usage of the words elsewhere. For this reason also I have translated *folklore* as 'folk culture' throughout, although 'the vernacular' would in some instances give his meaning greater contemporary vividness. The final decisions in this translation have all been my own, but I would like to acknowledge the help and advice of my father, Denzil I. Dunnett.

JAMES DUNNETT

40, rue de Villejust – XVIe

Sir,

    I have only one word to say about your book,* and it's a word I seldom use: admirable.

    And I write it with some embarrassment. My thoughts are at one with yours on most of the subjects you touch on. It is too easy for me to approve my own feelings.

    I may add that in literature, and even in philosophy, there are now analogous or coincidental points of view. But in these fields for insuperable reasons (too long to set out) one has to 'mesh' with the past. Buildings are seen by themselves and impose their presence on the observer, whereas what is written requires from the reader a willingness and good will, which depend on his expectations, and his expectations depend on his habits, etc. One cannot even make a start with the experience of purity except by bringing in the scattered examples of it to be found in the past.

    Believe me, sir, I hold your work in especial regard, and I am doing my best to make it known.

    With all my thanks and fellow-feeling,

(Signed) Paul Valéry

**L'Art décoratif d'aujourd'hui* (1925, *Collection de L'Esprit Nouveau*) published by Editions G. Crès, Paris.

PREFACE TO THE 1959 EDITION

Here is a letter from Paul Valéry, of 1925 (opposite).

●

Under this sign:

1925

**EXPO.
ARTS. DÉCO.**

about a dozen articles reflecting on the forthcoming 'International Exhibition of the Decorative Arts' had appeared in *L'Esprit Nouveau* (our international review of contemporary activity) during 1924. I did not sign the articles to avoid confusing the scene with personalities. A first series of articles from the 'E.N.' ('The Engineer's Aesthetic and Architecture', 'Three Reminders to Architects', 'Regulating Lines', 'Eyes which do not see', 'Architecture', 'Mass-Production Houses', 'Architecture or Revolution') had been brought together in 1923 in a book, *Vers une architecture*,[1] published by Crès. This was continuously reprinted until Crès ceased publication (in 1932). It was translated into English, German, Spanish, and Japanese. The series, the *Collection de L'Esprit Nouveau* was built up at Crès as follows: *Vers une architecture, L'Art décoratif d'aujourd'hui*,[2] *Urbanisme*,[3] *Almanach d'architecture moderne, Une Maison: un Palais, Précisions, Croisade*.

The 1925 Exhibition covered the Esplanade of the Invalides and the banks of the Seine from Concorde to Alma with constructions of plaster.

1. *Towards a New Architecture.* 2. *The Decorative Art of Today.* 3. *The City of Tomorrow.*

Plaster was king, and there was an astounding display of fancy and foliate
ornament. The exhibition left behind some '1925 Yearbooks' which spread
the style all over Paris and the rest of France.

We had undertaken to put up a pavilion of *L'Esprit Nouveau* which
would indissolubly link the equipment of the home (furniture) to architecture (the space inhabited, the dwelling), and to town-planning (the conditions of life of a society).

In face of a mass of difficulties – without a penny – we had put up the
Esprit Nouveau pavilion, built 'for real': an apartment from the *immeuble-
villas* ('villa-blocks') inspired in 1907 and 1910 by two visits to the Carthusian
monastery of Ema in Tuscany. Furniture as a mass-product for the mass, and
mass-produced objects: architectural plans linked to town-planning: architecture and town-planning making a UNITY, i.e. one and the same thing: a
diorama of 100 square metres ('A Contemporary City of 3 million inhabi-
tants' from the Salon d'Automne of 1922) and a second diorama 'The Voisin
Plan of Paris' (Gabriel Voisin having given us 25,000 francs and Henri
Frugès of Bordeaux having given us the other 25,000, making up the 50,000

The Pavilion of L'Esprit Nouveau, built from 'real' materials on the Cours de la Reine in 1925,
was a cell of human habitation.

The interior: a complete apartment in 'real' materials.

with which the Esprit Nouveau pavilion (by Le Corbusier and Pierre Jean-neret) was erected); it was in reinforced concrete, on two floors and with an area of 300 square metres. It stayed intact throughout the following winter, while as soon as the autumn of 1925 set in the plaster palaces started crumbling all over the Esplanade of the Invalides, the Pont Alexandre, and the banks of the Seine.

The International Grand Jury wanted to award us the Diploma of Honour of the Exhibition, but the President of the Jury (a great Frenchman) opposed it: 'There's no architecture in it!' he declared.*

●

This is the invitation card to the opening.

After overcoming all the snags, we were going to open our doors to the public. Then, one evening . . . we found that a palisade 7 metres high, painted green, had been put up, entirely hiding the Esprit Nouveau pavilion;

*This was Auguste Perret. J.I.D.

L'ESPRIT NOUVEAU

REVUE INTERNATIONALE DE L'ACTIVITÉ CONTEMPORAINE

LE CONSEIL D'ADMINISTRATION ET LA DIRECTION DE 'L'ESPRIT NOUVEAU'
LES 'AÉROPLANES G VOISIN' (AUTOMOBILES)
MR. HENRY FRUGES, DE BORDEAUX
LES ARCHITECTES LE CORBUSIER ET PIERRE JEANNERET

VOUS PRIENT DE LEUR FAIRE L'HONNEUR D'ASSISTER VENDREDI 10 JUILLET, A SEIZE HEURES,
A L'INAUGURATION DU PAVILLON DE L'ESPRIT NOUVEAU, SOUS LA PRÉSIDENCE DE
MONSIEUR DE MONZIE, MINISTRE DE L'INSTRUCTION PUBLIQUE ET DES BEAUX-ARTS.

LE PAVILLON DE L'ESPRIT NOUVEAU EST CONSACRÉ A LA RÉFORME DE L'HABITATION
(TRANSFORMATION DU PLAN, STANDARDISATION ET INDUSTRIALISATION). IL COMPORTE UNE CELLULE
ENTIÈRE DE ' L'IMMEUBLE-VILLAS ' AVEC JARDIN SUSPENDU ; DES ŒUVRES DE GEORGES BRAQUE,
JUAN GRIS, CH. E JEANNERET, FERÑAND LÉGER, JACQUES LIPCHITZ, AMÉDÉE OZENFANT,
PABLO PICASSO.

L'URBANISME DES GRANDES VILLES SERA EXPOSÉ SOUS FORME DES DIORAMAS D'UNE VILLE
CONTEMPORAINE DE 3 MILLIONS D'HABITANTS ET PRINCIPALEMENT DU PLAN ' VOISIN ' DE PARIS
(AMÉNAGEMENT DU CENTRE DE PARIS).

LE PAVILLON DE L'ESPRIT NOUVEAU EST SITUÉ DANS LE JARDIN ENTRE LES DEUX AILES
DU GRAND PALAIS, CÔTÉ COURS LA REINE, DERRIÈRE LE PAVILLON DU HAUT COMMISSARIAT

CE PAVILLON EST LE PLUS CACHÉ DE L'EXPOSITION

CETTE INVITATION TIENT LIEU DE CARTE D'ENTRÉE DANS L'EXPOSITION PAR LA PORTE D'HONNEUR
AVENUE ALEXANDRE III

this was by order of the Directorate of the Exhibition, which, moreover, charged us with the cost of putting it up . . .

The palisade came down, thanks to a Minister of National Education whose principal private secretary (whom we had got to come to the functions at our pavilion) has now become head of Electricité de France.

Inside the pavilion (in 1925) a fine placard announced: 'INDUSTRY TAKES OVER BUILDING' – the key premise.

In 1959, i.e. thirty-five years later, industry (AT LAST!) is taking over building . . .

L'ESPRIT NOUVEAU

TÉLÉPHONES
ÉLYSÉES) 44-97
) 44-08
) 46-07

LE NUMÉRO FRANCE : 6 Fr. »
              ÉTRANGER : 7 Fr. 50
ABONNEMENTS FRANCE : 70 Fr. »
              ÉTRANGER : 00 Fr. »

REVUE INTERNATIONALE ILLUSTRÉE DE L'ACTIVITÉ CONTEMPORAINE

35, Rue de Sèvres
SEXTES TÉLÉPHONES
PARIS (9ᵉ)
Le

EXPOSITION INTERNATIONALES DES ARTS DECORATIFS DE 1925

PAVILLON de " L'ESPRIT NOUVEAU "
Société Anonyme
Revue Internationale de l'Activité Contemporaine

SITUATION: Jardins du Grand Palais , sur le Cours La Reine

Ce pavillon reproduit rigoureusement l'une des cellules d'un grand immeuble locatif qui sera construit à Paris à partir de fin 1925.

Ce pavillon servira de démonstration

Ce pavillon par lui-même, constitue en soi, une villa qui sera érigée après l'Exposition en banlieue avec la presque totalité des éléments conçus démontables et transportables.

Ce pavillon constitue une démonstration saisissante des transformations radicales qui doivent être apportées dans la conception et dans les moyens constructifs du bâtiment; il est une illustration objective des théories parues dans la Revue l'ESPRIT NOUVEAU et dans ses éditions.

Ce pavillon sera vendu par adjudication au cours de l'exposition.

Suivant les conventions antérieures, les participants apportent leur concours gratuit, c'est à dire qu'ils fournissent gracieusement et abondonnent à la Société de l'ESPRIT NOUVEAU tout ce qui concerne leur collaboration.

●

The images included here* evoke the 1925 pavilion, which provided the occasion for the appearance of this book with its unassuming title: 'THE DECORATIVE ART OF TODAY.'

Paris, 1st May 1959   LE CORBUSIER

*Some of the illustrations which originally accompanied this preface have been omitted from this translation for reasons of space. They are readily available in volume 1 of the Œuvre Complète. J.I.D.

The pavilion of L'Esprit Nouveau incorporated into the framework of a Unité d'Habitation (1925).

The town planning section of the 1925 pavilion. The 'Plan Voisin' was the expression of a principle. This plan continued to evolve during the following thirty years.

P.S.
Page 106: a thousand apologies for the ill-treatment accorded to Rodin at the top of this page! But 'Paul' (the blasphemer) was at the age of rebellion and of discovery (p. 109) and also pages 112 (last paragraph) and 113 (first two paragraphs). But read also page (114), paragraph (2): 'A new desire . . .' He was burning what he had loved.

The shade of Rodin hasn't stirred!

My apologies have been made!

[Second] *P.S.*
On pages 193 to 214 the travel sketches of a young man of twenty to twenty-three are reproduced. He was searching the countryside and the towns for signs of the times, past and present, and learning as much from the work of ordinary mankind as from that of the great creative figures. It was in these encounters that he discovered architecture: *Where is architecture?* That was the question he asked unceasingly.

Page 99, third line. The phrase 'expressing the construction' (*accuser la construction*) means 'emphasizing the construction' (*mettre en valeur la construction*).

ARGUMENT

ICONOLOGY
ICONOLATERS
ICONOCLASTS

ICONS
ICONOLATERS

The past is not infallible . . . There were ugly things as well as beautiful . . .
'. . . An object of use should be decorated; as our companion in fortune and adversity it should have a soul. Together, the souls of objects that have been decorated create an atmosphere of warmth which brightens our unhappy lot. The great emptiness of the machine age should be countered by the ineffable diffusion of a soothing and gently intoxicating decoration.'

ICONOCLASTS

We protest.

The objects of utility in our lives have freed the slaves of a former age. They are in fact themselves slaves, menials, servants. Do you want them as your soulmates? We sit on them, work on them, make use of them, use them up; when used up, we replace them.

OTHER ICONS
THE MUSEUMS

The museums are a recent invention; previously there were none.
  In their tendentious incoherence, the museums provide no model; *they can offer only the elements of judgement.*
  The true museum would be one that contained everything, one able to

give the whole picture of a past age. Such a museum would be truly dependable and honest; its value would lie in the choice that it offered, whether to accept or reject; it would allow one to understand the reasons why things were as they were, and would be a stimulant to improve on them. Such a museum does not yet exist. Educationalists disregard, both in their books and in the schools, the origin and purpose of the objects in museums; they use them as the basis of their teaching, and urge on their pupils to outdo examples already exceptional of their kind, thus encouraging them to fill our lives with the impractical showpieces which clutter and distort our existence.

PLAGIARISM
FOLK CULTURE

Folk culture is a creation of the distant past, often dating back through many centuries. In the beginning, someone who was more of a poet than others in the crowd gave it expression; it made an impact. It was taken up. It was worked on, corrected, perfected to the level of human resources and emotions. It was polished. In order that it could be handed on, it was essential that its intentions were clear. It was clarified. It was confirmed ever more definitely in a meaning that became unanimous, and thereby transmissible.

We will become certain that the folk culture of today is in process of formation, indeed already exists, born of unanimous collaboration.

But the idle and sterile plagiarise the folk culture of the past, fill the air with the deafening cry of crickets, and sing out of tune with the poetry of others.

What effect will these resuscitations that they propose have on our lives? The resurrection of local cultures, the revival of the Langue d'Oc, Breton, or Tyrolean costume, the kimono or the peplum of Duncan, the pottery of Lunéville?

CONSEQUENCES OF THE CRISIS

The consequences of the crisis which has divided pre-machine society from the new industrial society are already upon us and are continuing to develop. Culture has taken a step forward and the hierarchical tradition of decoration has collapsed.

Gilding is fading out and the slums will not be with us long before they are abolished. Certainly, we appear to be working towards the establishment of a simple and economical human scale.

HURRICANE

One day the railway engine succeeded in setting the whole world in motion. It was the age of metals, the age of steel. *The steel in our hands was the machine; with the machine came calculation; with calculation, the solution of a hypothesis; with the solution of a hypothesis, the resolution of a dream. In the space of a hundred years, revolution was fomented: the industrial revolution, the social revolution, the moral revolution.*

Industry blew upon the world, and there was a hurricane.

The industrialist thought to himself: 'let us smother our junk with decoration: decoration hides all manner of flaws and blemishes'. The sanctifying of camouflage. Desperate inspiration and commercial triumph.

TYPE-NEEDS
TYPE-FURNITURE

To search for human scale, for human function, is to define human needs. These needs are 'type'. We all need means of supplementing our natural capabilities.

'Human-limb objects' are type objects responding to type needs.

Decorative Art is an inexact and wordy phrase by which we denote the totality of 'human-limb objects'. These respond with some precision to certain clearly established needs. Type-needs, type-functions, therefore type-objects and type-furniture.

The 'human-limb object' is a docile servant. A good servant is discreet and self-effacing, in order to leave his master free.

Works of decorative art are tools, beautiful tools.

THE DECORATIVE ART OF TODAY

Modern decorative art is not decorated.

But we are told that decoration is necessary to our existence. Let us correct that: art is necessary to us, that is to say, a disinterested passion that exalts us.

So, to see things clearly, it is sufficient to separate the satisifaction of disinterested emotion from that of utilitarian need. Utilitarian needs call for tools, brought in every respect to that degree of perfection seen in industry. This then is the great programme for the decorative arts. Day after day industry is turning out tools of perfect utility and convenience that soothe our spirits with the luxury afforded by the elegance of their conception, the purity of their execution, and the efficiency of their operation.

This rational perfection and this precise formulation constitute sufficient common ground between them to allow the recognition of a style.

THE LESSON OF THE MACHINE

The machine, a recent phenomenon, is bringing about a reformation of the spirit across the world.

Nevertheless, the human factor remains intact, since the machine was invented by man to serve human needs.

The machine is conceived not in the realms of fantasy but within the spiritual framework which man has constructed for himself – a framework which forms his tangible universe. This framework, wrested element by element from the world around us, is sufficiently cogent to permit the creation of organisms performing functions similar to those of the natural world.

The machine is all geometry. Geometry is our greatest creation and we are enthralled by it.

The machine brings before us shining disks, spheres, and cylinders of polished steel, shaped with a theoretical precision and exactitude which can never be seen in nature itself. *Our senses are moved, and at the same time our heart recalls from its stock of memories the disks and spheres of the gods of Egypt and the Congo. Geometry and gods sit side by side!*

Man pauses before the machine, and the beast and the divine in him there eat their fill.

The lesson of the machine lies in the pure relationship of cause and effect. Purity, economy, the reach for wisdom. A new desire: an aesthetic of purity, of exactitude, of expressive relationships setting in motion the mathematical mechanisms of our spirit: a spectacle and a cosmogony.

RESPECT FOR WORKS OF ART

Decorative art can no longer exist any more than can the 'styles' themselves. In relation to the style of an age, the styles are no more than an accidental surface modality, superadded to facilitate composition, stuck on to disguise faults, or duplicated for the sake of display.

If decorative art has no reason to exist, tools on the other hand do exist, and there exist also architecture and the work of art.

A tool, something that gives service, a servant, a menial. One single requirement: that it serves well.

Architecture is a construct of the mind which gives material form to the sum consciousness of its age.

The work of art, the living 'double' of a being, whether still present, or departed, or unknown; that moment of profound discourse; those open and eloquent words spoken in the intimacy of the soul; perhaps this Sermon on the Mount.

Decorative art departs far from these paths; to attempt to define its position is to reveal clearly its purpose and its quite different orientation: that of providing decoration, of upholding decorum.

The work of art grows ever more concentrated.
We feel ourselves disposed to respect the work of art.
The hour of architecture sounds, now that art awaits the spiritual expression of our age in material form, now that decorative art can no longer be considered acceptable within the framework of contemporary aspiration.

THE HOUR OF ARCHITECTURE

Great art lives by humble means.
Glitter is going under.
The hour of proportion has arrived.
The spirit of architecture is asserting itself.
What has occurred? The machine age has been born.
Our effusions, and our vivid appreciation of the beauties and power of nature have found their place within the framework of architecture. For science, by revealing to us the phenomenon of the universe, has placed great creative power in our hands, and architecture is the necessary condition for human creation.

MILESTONES

The Eiffel Tower has been accepted as architecture.
In 1889, it was seen as the aggressive expression of mathematical calculation.
In 1900, the aesthetes wanted to demolish it.
In 1925, it dominated the Exhibition of Modern Decorative Arts. Above the plaster palaces writhing with decoration, it stood out pure as crystal.

THE SENSE OF TRUTH

Even before the formulation of a theory, the emotion leading to action can be felt: theory later gives support to sentiment in a variety of seemingly incontrovertible ways.
An active being carries with him the sense of truth, which is his power of judgement. It is an imperative which is at the same time his force and lucidity. The sense of truth is the strength of a man.
In respect of our work, of human labour, of the human world, nothing exists or has the right to exist that has no explanation. We set to work: our intention must be clear because we are not madmen. We work for a purpose . . . however crass it may be.
I notice that a whole mass of objects which once bore the sense of truth have lost their content and are now no more than carcasses: I throw them out.

I will throw everything out from the past except that which is still of service to me. Some things are always of service: art.

A COAT OF WHITEWASH
THE LAW OF RIPOLIN

We all confront the problem of our surroundings for the sake of our comfort and well-being, for the delight of our hearts, for our pleasure, and also for the satisfaction of a feeling for what is fitting: we would like to be appropriate. *Elimination of the equivocal. Concentration of intention on its proper object, and attention on* the *object. An object is held to be made only out of necessity, for a specific purpose, and to be made with perfection. A perfect object is a living organism, animated by the sense of truth.*

Suppose we concede to decorative art the care of our sentient being. Let us accept this proposition. We thus make ourselves judges of matters of sensibility. It would be a valuable achievement indeed to make each one of us a prudent judge. In the confusion of our tumultuous times many have become accustomed to think against a background of black. But the tasks of our century, so strenuous, so full of danger, so violent, so victorious, seem to demand of us that we think against a background of white.

1925

EXPO.
ARTS. DÉCO.

1

The past is not infallible . . . There were ugly things as well as beautiful . . .

'. . . An object of use should be decorated: as our companion in fortune and adversity it should have a soul. Together, the souls of objects that have been decorated create an atmosphere of warmth which brightens our unhappy lot. The great emptiness of the machine age should be countered by the ineffable diffusion of a soothing and gently intoxicating decoration.'

We protest.

The objects of utility in our lives have freed the slaves of a former age. They are in fact themselves slaves, menials, servants. Do you want them as your soul-mates? We sit on them, work on them, make use of them, use them up; when used up, we replace them.

An ostrich.

ICONOLOGY
ICONOLATERS
ICONOCLASTS

ICONOLOGY

Coaches are on the move along the highways of Europe. Escorts with pistols in their saddle-holsters, etc.

L.P. Phot.   Versailles.

The tyrants have decided to send ambassadors to say hello to the GREAT KING.

The ambassador is getting excited as he approaches his goal. He is oblivious of the deeply rutted roads, the plains scoured by the wind, the treacherous defiles.

The Italian: This table that I have brought from Florence is the summit of art; a rare present. Crafty old mosaicists and goldsmiths, you have managed with your rare stones, unearthed in the far corners of the ancient empire (Caesar's!), to make a most ridiculous bauble, a most disturbing contrivance; this polished surface is plunged in the deepest waters, trees glitter, rocks shine, the sky glows, jade, jasper, onyx, agate, lapis, crystal.

The emissary of Catherine the Great: This gigantic vase, hewn from a single stone, will win me the treaty. Oh most rich Urals! Mongol Urals! Asiatic Urals! Malachite, pure gold! Pure gold, malachite! THE GREAT KING. That will do the trick!

From Ethiopia, Damascus, Teheran, and elsewhere: 'Look at that fire, those shafts of light, those stars! a crystallization of natural marvels: the blue sea, the green lake, the snow on the mountain tops, the sun, the sky over the

L.P. Phot.   Fontainebleau.

Pyramids (exclusively laudatory metaphors!). Their eyes roll, focus, and then roll again; their eyelids flutter, tears roll. *Tenderly: With that one can do business.*

Etc., etc.

The coaches bump along in the ruts, nature is grey, without malachite, pure gold, or metaphors.

At the palace of the GREAT KING.

The Minister of Ceremonies: 'Ah, the things they're going to see!

'True enough, the park is lousy, like a vine in winter, with its stakes. It's young, but it'll grow. The palace, magnificent! What expense! He said: gold, marble, mirrors, everywhere! Let thousands of bronzes be cast and gilded with pure gold. Let the walls be buried beneath festoons, panelling, cameos, paintings. After ours, no one will talk any longer of the Doges' ceilings. Let there be axes, he decreed. And axes were laid out like the rays of the sun. Inlaid floors were spread out like carpets of stone. Doorframes were bedecked with every kind of carving that timber can sustain, and then a leaf of pure gold on top of that. Walls of precious stone interspaced with mirrors. His Majesty portrayed by the greatest masters, in gold. And then the chandeliers with their hundred thousand candles. Ah, let the ambassadors come!'

(Beginning to tire.) – 'Hey you, valets, waxers, polishers, upholsterers! get rubbing, and make sure it glows!'

The King enters, with a coiffure of ostrich feathers, in red, canary, and pale blue; ermine, silk, brocade, and lace; a cane of gold, ebony, ivory, and diamonds.

– 'Your Majesty!'

Pausing, contentment in his eyes, and with a smile: 'By G–, murmured the KING, talking to himself, we're going to stun them!'

* * *

ICONOLATERS

Certainly courtiers, princelings, squires, aimed at much the same thing in their own spheres, even though it might be with impure gold and imitation marble.

Marat appeared, and tried to establish the decent conventions of the Citizen; but he died, the Citizen with him.

The Bourgeois King adorned his close-stool with foliage and his wall-papers with damask. Impure gold gave way to powdered brass.

The Bourgeois Republican decorated his stove with foliage; casting for casting, the price was the same as plain – so much a kilo; what a godsend!

The professor of the Republican School for the Applied Arts: 'Young'uns, called as you will be one day to further the glory of salt cellars, baldacchinos, and dressing tables, be off with you to the museums and royal castles, to absorb the sublime lesson of those wonderful periods . . . alas no longer with us (sobs).'

Publishers and booksellers of France and abroad: 'My word, we could certainly keep ourselves busy for quite a while publishing luxury, semi-luxury, and popular editions of the wonders in the museums and country houses, the sublime lessons of those wonderful periods . . . re-awake the memory of those periods . . . fortunately abolished by the march of progress and lost in oblivion (no sobs).'

Agreement between the paper merchants and the book industries in general.

The writers on art join in and buy goose quills.

The public learns, and is dazzled. Diamonds, pure gold, foliate orna-ment, marbles, and mirrors; that titillates all right: 'Good Lord, how rich, how beautiful (consecutive and synonymous exclamations). And all made by hand!' The intoxicated public plunges vertiginously into the beauties of the past. Wonderful periods, long gone. Sincere and innocent regrets. We can't do that anymore! (sincere sobs).

The Faubourg Saint-Antoine* stands together as one man: 'Cheer up, we'll make it for you, and it won't be too expensive!'

Antiquarians play their part (like Sunday chemists) in keeping the sacred flame alight in the temple.

Nobility keeps watch, seated in its genuine armchairs.

**

The professors at the schools, royal or republican,
    the keepers and labellers in the museums,
    the publishers in France and abroad,
    the writers on art,
    the Faubourg Saint-Antoine,
    the antiquarians,
    the annual salons, the displays in shops and department stores,
    the public finally ground down, instructed, exhorted, softened up, converted, credulous and 'au fait', all of them, clergy and catechumens of the new faith, have decided: *an object of use should be decorated; as our companion in fortune and adversity it should have a soul. Together, the souls of objects that have been decorated create an atmosphere of warmth which brightens our unhappy lot. The great emptiness of the machine age should be countered by the ineffable diffusion of a soothing and gently intoxicating decoration.*

Hold on a moment, coldly: 'Decoration? I don't understand, I don't know what you mean. Decoration, why? Decoration, by my life and soul, why? Decoration, by all that's good, why?'

It is a religion, with an imposing body of clergy: 'IT'S ART', they reply, the whole body of iconolaters replies.

That's the end of your protest, sir!

**

ICONOCLASTS

We now make our protest and offer our explanation.

Lenin is seated at the Rotonde on a cane chair;[1] he has paid twenty centimes for his coffee, with a tip of one sou. He has drunk out of a small white porcelain cup. He is wearing a bowler hat and a smooth white collar. He has been writing for several hours on sheets of typing paper. His inkpot is smooth and round, made from bottle glass.

*The mass-market furniture district of Paris. J.I.D.

1. The scene is set before the war.

Phot. X.   Louis XIV, by Rigaud.

He is teaching himself to govern one hundred million people.

We protest in the name of everything. In the name of happiness, in the name of well-being, in the name of reason, in the name of culture, in the name of morality, in the name of good taste, in the name of our ancestors whose work we respect.

The objects of utility in our lives have freed the slaves of a former age. They are in fact themselves slaves, menials, servants. Do you want them as your soul-mates? We sit on them, work on them, use them up; when used up, we replace them.

L'Illustré. Khai Dinh, the present emperor of Annam.

We demand from such servants precision and care, decency, and an unassertive presence.

The past is not infallible . . . There were ugly things as well as beautiful. Bad taste was not born yesterday. The past has one advantage over the present: we have half forgotten it. The interest we take in it does not excite our active energies, which are violently engaged in the contemporary world, but it soothes our hours of leisure; we contemplate it with the benevolence of disinterest. Ethnographic significance, documentary importance, historical value, collectable value, all these are superimposed on its beauty or ugliness

M. Gaston Doumergue, President of the French Republic.

and, in either case, add to our interest. Our admiration for the artefacts of an earlier culture is thus often objective, a captivating encounter by our animal spirit with its own image lingering in the products of a developing culture: the simple human animal of a fun fair. Culture is a progression towards the

L'Illustré. The opening of the English parliament. The king and queen.

The dictionary of the styles over the ages, and the bric-à-brac of our own times.

inner life. Gilt decoration and precious stones are the work of the tamed savage who is still alive in us.

No practical or elevated argument excuses or explains iconolatry. Since iconolatry thrives and spreads as virulently as a cancer, let us be iconoclasts.

1925

EXPO.

ARTS. DÉCO.

2

The museums are a recent creation and previously there were none.

In their tendentious incoherence the museums provide no model; *they can offer only the elements of judgement.*

The true museum is one that contains everything, one able to give the whole picture of a past age. Such a museum would be truly dependable and honest; its value would lie in the choice that it offered, whether to accept or reject; it would allow one to understand the reasons why things were as they were, and would be a stimulant to improve on them. Such a museum does not yet exist.

Educationalists disregard, both in their books and in the schools, the origin and purpose of the objects in museums; they use them as the basis of their courses, and urge on their pupils to outdo examples already exceptional of their kind, thus encouraging them to fill our lives with the impractical showpieces which clutter and distort our existence.

Maison Pirsoul.

OTHER ICONS
THE MUSEUMS

There are good museums, and bad. Then there are those with the good and bad together. But the museum is a sacred entity which debars judgement.

The birth of the museum: 100 years ago; the age of humanity: 40 or 400,000 years.

To see your happy smile, dear lady, as you say 'My daughter is at the museum', you would appear to feel you are one of the pillars of the world!

The museums are a recent invention; once there were none. So let us admit that they are not a fundamental component of human life like bread, drink, religion, orthography.

True enough, there is good in the museums; but let us risk a devastating deduction: the museum allows one to reject it all, because once the full story is known, it becomes clear that everything has its time and place and that nothing from the past is directly of use to us. For our life on this world is a path on which we can never retrace out steps. This is so clear that I can conclude with an immutable law: in their tendentious incoherence, the museums provide no model; they offer only the elements of judgement. The strong in spirit always get out of them, they understand and recognize the poison, and the opiate does not interest them; they see clearly, and do not slide pitifully down the precipice.

But should social reality be considered only in terms of the strong in spirit? It is a dangerous limitation. The phenomenon of nature manifests itself in the form of a pyramid, a hierarchy: at the summit there are the aces; lower down in ever-increasing waves, those of less excellent, inferior quality. The ratio is quickly evident: for every 10 units of height there is a single example of excellence at the summit and 100 of middling or mediocre quality at the bottom; for 100 units of height there are 10 of excellence at the top and 10,000 mediocrities at the bottom, etc., and the space in between is occupied by the mass of intermediate quality. Those at the top are supported there by the presence of the lower levels, graded in ascending order.

The pyramid expresses a hierarchy. Hierarchy is the organisational law of the world, both natural and human.

So it is important to consider whether the museums help or hinder appreciation of the principle of hierarchical gradation.

THE MUSEUM REVEALS THE FULL STORY, AND IT IS THERE-FORE GOOD: IT ALLOWS ONE TO CHOOSE, TO ACCEPT OR REJECT.

Let us imagine a true museum, one that contained everything, one that could present a complete picture after the passage of time, after the destruction by time (and how well it knows how to destroy! so well, so completely, that almost nothing remains except objects of great show, of great vanity, of great fancy, which always survive disasters, testifying to vanity's indestructible powers of survival). In order to flesh out our idea, let us put together a museum of our own day with objects of our own day; to begin:

A plain jacket, a bowler hat, a well-made shoe. An electric light bulb with bayonet fixing; a radiator, a table cloth of fine white linen; our everyday drinking glasses, and bottles of various shapes (Champagne, Bordeaux) in which we keep our Mercurey, our Graves, or simply our *ordinaire* . . . A number of bentwood chairs with caned seats like those invented by Thonet of Vienna, which are so practical that we use them ourselves as much as do our employees. We will install in the museum a bathroom with its enamelled bath, its china bidet, its wash-basin, and its glittering taps of copper or nickel. We will put in an Innovation suitcase and a Roneo filing cabinet with its printed index cards, tabulated, numbered, perforated, and indented, which will show that in the twentieth century we have learnt how to classify. We will also put in those fine leather armchairs of the types developed by Maples: beneath them we might place a label saying: 'These armchairs, invented at the beginning of the XXth century, were a real innovation in the art of furniture design; furthermore, they were a good example of intelligent research into comfort: but at that time what was done best was not yet what was most highly prized; bizarre and expensive furniture was still preferred which constituted an index of all the kinds of carving and colouring that had graced the more showy furniture of earlier epochs.' In this section of the museum we would have no hesitation in displaying other labels explaining that all objects on exhibition had performed some real function; in this way one would come to appreciate a new phenomenon characteristic of this period, namely that the objects of utility used by the rich and by the poor were not very different from one another, and varied only in their finish and quality of manufacture.

Clearly, this museum does not yet exist. Such a museum would be truly dependable and honest; its value would lie in the choice that it offered, whether to approve or reject; it would allow one to understand the reasons why things were as they were and would be a stimulant to improve on them.

Tourists on their way to climb Vesuvius sometimes stop in the museums of Pompeii and Naples, and there they eagerly look at the sarcophagi incrusted with ornament.

But Pompeii, as a result of a miraculous event, constitutes the single true museum worthy of the name. To confirm its value for the education of the masses, one can only hope to see the immediate establishment of a second Pompeian museum, of the modern epoch: societies have already been formed for this purpose; they have put together the displays in the Pavillon de Marsan, the museum of contemporary decorative arts; there they certainly give some indication of the present century, but it is only partial and fragmentary. The inhabitant of another planet who suddenly landed there would be more likely to think he was at Charenton.*

*The well-known lunatic asylum. J.I.D.

Photo Giraudon.   Pavillon de Marsan.

THE MUSEUM IS BAD BECAUSE IT DOES NOT TELL THE WHOLE STORY. IT MISLEADS, IT DISSIMULATES, IT DELUDES. IT IS A LIAR.

The objects that are put in the showcases of our museums are sanctified by this fact: they are said to be collectable, to be rare and precious – valuable, and therefore beautiful. They are pronounced beautiful and held up as models, and thus is established that fatal chain of ideas and their consequences. Where do they come from? From the churches, ever since these espoused magnificence to dazzle, impress, attract, and impose respect for an omnipotent deity. God was in the gold and in the carving; He had failed to keep an appointment with St Francis of Assisi and, many centuries later, had still not come down into the suburbs of our 'tentacle cities'.

These objects also came from the palaces and country houses: to impress, astound, appease the gaudy Punch who jerks somewhere in us all and whom culture catches, ties up and muzzles. We feel very indulgent

Museum of Decorative Arts, Paris.

towards the distant past; we are full of indulgence and very ready to find
everything good and beautiful, we who afterwards are so critical of the disinterested and passionate efforts of our contemporaries. We forget too easily
that bad taste was not born yesterday; without extensive research, but
simply by sticking one's nose into a few old tomes from the eighteenth
century, one can become well aware that even at that time people of good
taste and position were continually protesting against the profligacy of the
arts and crafts, and against the manufacturers of rubbish.

At the Bibliotèque Nationale there is valuable evidence of the
decadence that has sometimes been rife, for example: *Fashionable Architecture, Including the Latest Designs for the Decoration of Buildings and Gardens, by the Best Architects, Sculptors, Gardeners, Locksmiths, etc., at Paris,
published by Langlois.*

And also *Designs for Various Ornaments and Mouldings, Antique and
Modern, Suitable for Architecture, Painting, Sculpture, Goldsmithing,
Embroidery, Marquetry, Damask, Joinery, Locksmithing and Other Arts,
with the Name of Each Ornament.*

There, engraved on copper, are the most revealing ornaments, the most useless knick-knacks which the Faubourg Saint-Antoine has been able to produce; their date is 1700–1750, Louis XIV–Louis XV.

A Book of Mirrors, Tables and Pedestal-tables designed by Lepautre, A Book of Scroll Ornaments Newly Designed and Engraved by Jean d'Olivar and sold in Paris by Langlois, with the Authority of the King.

Among the chimney-pieces of imitation marble and pier glasses of gilt icing sugar, some have angels, some crowns, some medallions, etc.

What a collection to send the world of its time to sleep! It makes one feel that the bourgeois must date from before the Revolution. The utter lack of taste is stupefying.

In addition there are twenty plates, each one with about thirty friezes, gadroons, rosettes, scotias, astragals, volutes, fleurons, plinths, echini, acanthus leaves, etc. And all this is disgustingly drawn, cheap rubbish, designed as announced, for the engraver and architect, and for the painter. And the architects certainly took their pick, with the expected results: a great deal of old furniture laden with brass ornament, etc. And on what principle are these albums organised? Each plate is divided into four quarters along its two main axes; on either side of the axes there are four segments of mirror, four segments of vase, four segments of chimney-piece, etc. One can

Photo Giraudon.   Musée de Cluny.

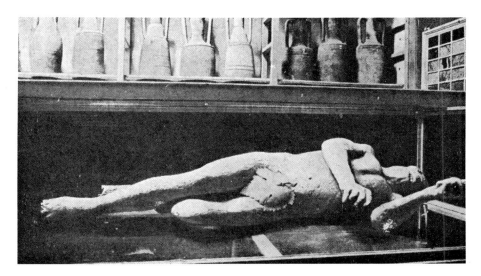

Museum at Pompeii.

see the matching up from here! Catalogues of monumental masonry are better presented today.

And where have the objects made from these elements ended up? In the homes of high society, with collectors, with antiquarians, and in the museums. Inevitably in such a heap there are some very beautiful things. But what is undeniable is our own automatic admiration and total loss of critical faculties when it comes to the heritage of past centuries. Who was this job lot from the reign of the great kings intended for? For a kind of person for whom we do not have much respect today; so it is disastrous and almost immoral to send our children into the museums to learn a religious respect for objects that are ill-made and offensive. And here again the Conservators would do us an immense service if they agreed to display labels alongside their exhibits declaring for example: 'This armchair or this commode would have belonged to a parvenu grocer living in about 1750, etc.'

The honest ethnographic museum is itself incomplete. This can be explained, and therefore excused: a colonial deep in the virgin forest prefers to bring back, in the limited space available, an object of display belonging to a negro chief or the local deity, rather than to encumber himself with numerous utensils that would give a picture of the cultural condition of the peoples with whom he has come into contact. Admittedly, we are at least as keen that the colonial should bring back the image of a god from the virgin forest as a calabash which served as a bowl or a bottle. But where this question becomes serious is when our educationalists, both in their books and in the schools, disregard the origin and purpose of the objects displayed in the museums, and use them as the basis of their teaching, to urge on their pupils to outdo, if that is possible, examples already exceptional of their kind, and thus encourage them to fill our everyday lives with the impractical showpieces which clutter and distort our existence, leaving it quite simply ridiculous.

ICONOCLASTS AGAIN: MAN, MAN QUITE NAKED.

The naked man does not wear an embroidered waistcoat; so the saying goes!

The naked man – but he is an animal worthy of respect who, feeling a head with a brain on his shoulders, sets himself to achieve something in the world.

The naked man sets himself to think, and by developing his tools, seeks to free himself from the dominance of external circumstance and the necessity for exhausting labour. He uses his tools to make objects of utility, and the purpose of these objects is to lighten the unpleasant tasks of everyday life.

The naked man, once he is fed and housed . . . and clothed, sets his mind to work and focuses his thoughts on what he thinks best and most noble.

The fabulous development of the book, of print, and the classification of the whole of the most recent archaeological era, have flooded our minds and overwhelmed us. We are in an entirely new situation: *Everything is known to us*. Peoples, periods, apogees, declines. We even know the shape of the cranium of the contemporaries of the dinosaurs, and from the slope of the forehead the thoughts which must have occupied them. Whenever a problem arises, we can apply exhaustive analysis to conjure up a picture of what any peoples did or would have done at any period. Ours is certainly an era of documentation.

But the museums have made the arbitrary choice that I have just denounced; this warning should be engraved on their pediments: 'Within will be found the most partial, the least convincing documentation of past ages; remember this and be on your guard!' Truth is thus re-established, and we can proceed without further comment to our own very different programme. Our own purpose is not to imitate the weaknesses of the weaker classes of earlier ages; we intend our culture to serve some purpose, and spur us on to the best. The museums are a means of instruction for the most intelligent, just as the city of Rome is a fruitful lesson for those who have a profound knowledge of their craft.

Musée de Saint-Germain-en-Laye.

The naked man does not wear an embroidered waistcoat; he wishes to think. The naked man is a normally constituted being, who has no need of trinkets. His mechanism is founded on logic. He likes to understand the reasons for things. It is the reasons that bring light to his mind. He has no prejudices. He does not worship fetishes. He is not a collector. He is not the keeper of a museum. If he likes to learn, it is to arm himself. He arms himself to attack the task of the day. If he likes occasionally to look around himself and behind himself in time, it is in order to grasp the reasons why. And when he finds harmony, this thing that is a creation of his spirit, he experiences a shock that moves him, that exalts him, that encourages him, that provides him with support in life.

1925

EXPO.
ARTS. DÉCO.

3

Folk culture is a creation of the distant past, often dating back through many ages. In the beginning, someone who was more of a poet than others in the crowd gave it expression; it made an impact. It was taken up. It was worked on, corrected, perfected to the level of human resources and emotions. It was polished. In order that it could be handed on, it was essential that its intentions were clear. It was clarified. It was confirmed ever more definitely in a meaning that became unanimous, and therefore transmissible.

We will grow certain that the folk culture of today *is in process of formation, indeed already exists, born of unanimous collaboration.*

But the idle and sterile plagiarise the folk culture of the past, fill the air with the deafening cry of crickets, and sing out of tune with the poetry of others.

What effect will these resuscitations that they propose have on our lives? The resurrection of local cultures, the revival of the Langue d'Oc, Breton or Tyrolean costume, the kimono or the peplum of Duncan, the pottery of Lunéville?

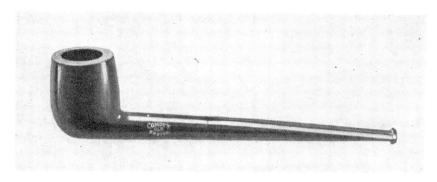

Comoy's pipe.

PLAGIARISM
FOLK CULTURE

To be idle, void of ideas, to have a bric-à-brac mind, to be one of the crowd, the *bourgeois*-king of today, and quite openly to *despoil*, without pretence or verbal disguise, a neighbouring race engaged like its fathers and ancestors in conceiving works of perfect precision, and in finishing them with admirable and unwearying attention to detail. To be *Ubu-Roi* and to exclaim with gestures that sweep the stage: 'Folk culture, not bad, eh? I'll have some!' Plagiarism. Argentine tangos, Louisiana jazz, Russian embroidery, Breton

Etruria.

wardrobes, faience from almost everywhere, *Japonaiserie* of all kinds – a sentimental and decorative hubbub, quite *ersatz*, which rustles as we move, bathing us in P-o-e-t-r-y . . . invented by others and filling whatever empty holes may be left in our crowded days.

Polynesia.

The cinema, the café, the theatre, the stadium, the club, the 'five o'clock', suppers, dance halls, domestic wireless – all are diversions which flourish in exact proportion to the amount of leisure permitted by daily work; 'Good Lord, I hope we won't be all by ourselves!' is a common enough thought, expressed by people terrified at the prospect of having to fill time alone with their own thoughts for 1 hour, 2 hours, 3 hours. Miraculously, daily work provides marching orders of Prussian rigour; blinkers so one can't see, shafts to keep order, and a whip behind and on the behind to maintain contact with guiding intelligence. Such is daily work, which seems like the galleys, and which no one likes very much because they are kept at it by

Peru.

means of blows on the behind. But they do not feel alone; they do not feel on the shelf; they are happy to be in an office where discipline reigns, where everything is organised – to feel themselves firmly between the shafts, on all four feet and with blinkers on, and with the babble of Tartarin all round – the chamber music of Erik Satie.

First of all *regularity*, our daily bread.

Then *background noise* to fill in the holes, the emptiness. Musical noise, coloured noise, embroidered or batiked noise. A low volume of noise, a high volume of noise, reading the newspaper (description of the actions of others), cinemas, dance-halls, Pigall's . . . in order to get away from oneself, never be alone. 'If I were to come face to face with my soul (fearful thought)? What would I say to it? Watch out!'

Thus they keep their distractions on the go to avoid having to face themselves.

The antiquities of the antiquarian, the gilded palaces of the Kings, the

Renaissance.

museums of the peacock's feather, and finally the poetry of folk culture – a ready source of such distractions – all provide an opportunity to avoid confronting oneself, to evade the need to create. To create? Yes, that is to say, to put two ideas *of one's own* together, and then to continue: four ideas, eight ideas, etc. Time passes and this introspection, this continuity of thought, makes each man free, with his own powers of judgement, and ready for all the joys of exploring his own freedom; infinity is open to him. Yes, but that can induce vertigo!

The idle plagiarise the folk culture of the past, fill the air with the deafening cry of crickets, and sing out of tune with the poetry of others.

* * *

If we try to imagine how folk cultures are formed, we will grow certain that the *folk culture of today* is in process of formation, indeed already exists, born of unanimous collaboration. We will be convinced that a work of perfection, of value, of lasting quality, conforming to our needs and reflecting our thoughts, is being built every day from the vigour and powers of inven-

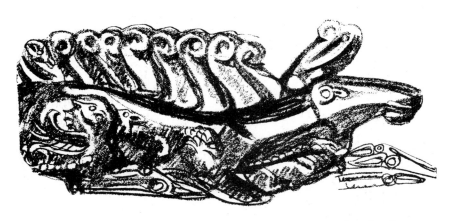

Scandinavia.

tion of us all; all tawdry ornament will seem laughable to us, and we will make up our minds to be well rid of it; we will want to wash ourselves and to cease meeting each other rigged out in moth-eaten cast-offs and lousy wigs.

I hear a czarda over the Serbian Danube; at a gymnastic display I listen to eight sturdy fellows sing the most beautiful mountain airs. At the *Cuadro Flamenco* of the Diaghilev Ballet eight Spaniards dance and sing; forty negroes of the *Syncopated Orchestra* gesticulate and fill one with nostalgia.

Throughout, all is clean, concise, brief, economical, intense, essential. It is immediately comprehensible to me, I feel it, and I experience exactly the intended emotion. A line has been etched; I see it and I remember. The trigger-action is precise: in my heart a particular compartment responds to the emotion, a standard emotion, an emotion so standard that immediately I throw out bridges: one leads to the corresponding period that is recognised as a stage; another leads to the realm of sun or of cloud; another to the arena of bitterness or of trust, of joys or anxieties; another carries me to the kingdom of the powers of good, and another to that of the powers of evil. At the meeting point of all these bridges there is a man. The climates, the suns, the regimes, the races, everything is classified in terms of its relationship to man. A typical, standardised, normal man: two legs, two arms, a head. A man who perceives red, or blue, or yellow, or green; a man who dreams of verticals or horizontals; a man who loves or who hates, who fondles or fights; a man who dances because he is happy.

These melodies, or equally these vases, these fetishes, these houses are

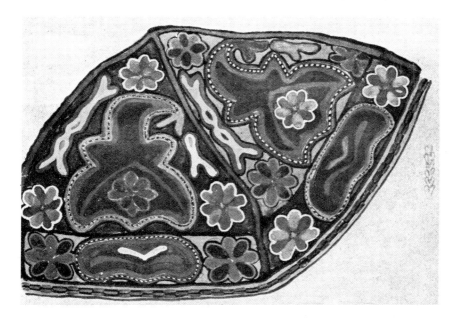

Russia.

not the work of a certain Mr X. They are a creation of the distant past, often dating back through many ages. In the beginning, someone who was more of a poet than others in the crowd gave expression to the idea; it made an impact. It was taken up. It was worked on, corrected, perfected to the level of human resources and emotions. It was polished. In order that it could be handed on, it was essential that its intentions were clear. It was clarified. It was confirmed ever more definitely in a meaning that became unanimous, and thereby transmissible. At last it became the perfect mirror of its people: an Alp or the sea could see its own image in the eye of a man.

Serbian

Folk culture in its lyric power. The lapse of centuries would bring Pegasus round again. The river, the tree, the flowers are transcribed into essential forms. Overflowing poetic feeling, whose expression has been fixed for centuries, makes this vase an outstanding artefact. The Serbian potter who made it in about 1900 had stowed it away with many others in his attic. The shelves of his house were filled with commercial pottery decorated in a vulgar way by machine. 'Progress' had brutally crippled age-old traditions. But he continued to turn out jars for every-day use similar to this Spanish jar, and also similar to the Adrianople jars which themselves resembled Greek amphoras. But some weeks later, all round the Aegean coast, I saw that the jars and amphoras once used to fetch water from the well (as they had been for two thousand years) had been superseded and that the potter was no longer at work. Tin petrol cans from

Spanish.

Batum were proving very convenient containers, besides being unbreakable. Instead of carrying the jar (just the jar) on one's shoulder, by taking the top off a petrol can and putting a piece of wood across it, one could carry its five litres as easily as one carries a suitcase. With a can in each hand one was balanced and did twice the work. What about the immortal pose of Ruth at Jacob's well and the really beautiful industry of the potter which seems to have been the companion of civilisation since time began? *Finished*! Replaced by a tin can. This story from the land of fine culture and imperishable art contains one of the most powerful lessons to be learnt today: evolution due to economics is inexorable and irresistible; regret is useless; poetry which seemed immortal is dead; everything begins again; that is what is fine and promises the joys of tomorrow.

Folk culture is a magnificent creation. An achievement purified by time and number.

Can one imagine that a single individual, in most cases lacking technical precision, could achieve such perfection with the daub of a brush?

Folk culture is so powerful that we all immediately respond to it; if offers the broadest channel for the expression of the mind and the heart.

Whether Tartar, Romanian, Scandinavian, Negro, or Bavarian, it holds past ages within itself.

'Omega' watch.

Our present era has not abandoned all effort. On the contrary, it has begun work under the influence of new stimuli, stimuli of a force hitherto unknown. For folk culture is a perfect expression of the physical and emotional resources of a people, and the peoples of today, united in a single immense confederation, have stunning physical resources at their disposal which have nothing in common with those of earlier periods. And as a result, since new means are available, new needs never satisfied before are clamouring for new solutions.

Work has begun. The unanimity of the new sense of feeling, which reflects an epoch of precision dominated by the machine, is tending to establish standards which will be our own folk culture. Problems tackled on a large scale. Abandonment of regional characteristics in favour of an international character. Frontiers fall and the whole surface of the world is known to us; only man remains intact with his clearly defined needs and an enlarged sense of poetry. What effect will these resuscitations that they propose have on our lives? The resurrection of local cultures, the revival of the Langue d'Oc, Breton or Tyrolean costume, the kimono or the peplum of Duncan, the pottery of Lunéville?

That has all been overtaken, shelved, superseded by the new sense of feeling. To react is to look backwards, and also to break oneself up like a tree fallen in the torrent.

Such anachronistic diversions may tickle the fancy of Monsieur Homais,* who furnished his mantelpiece with two Japanese vases from the *Compagnie des Indes*. Down with Monsieur Homais! We must see clearly and concern ourselves with the affairs of the present.

*The chemist in Flaubert's *Madame Bovary*. J.I.D.

1925

EXPO.

ARTS. DÉCO.

4

The consequence of the crisis which has divided pre-machine society from the new industrial society are already upon us and are continuing to develop.

Culture has taken a step forward and the hierarchical tradition of decoration has collapsed.

Gilding is fading out and the slums will not be with us long before they are abolished.

Certainly, we appear to be working towards the establishment of a simple and economical human scale.

Chair by Thonet (inventor of the bent wood chair).

CONSEQUENCES OF THE CRISIS

'You have suppressed everything that money can provide.' 25 March 1923.[1]

Yes, our present crisis certainly has its consequences. Culture has taken a step forward and the hierarchical system of decoration has collapsed. The participation of everyone in daily work has blasted obstacles from our path;

1. This was the assertion of Mr M— to his son who was moving into a new home in Paris. The younger Mr M— is an American whose means would have permitted him to furnish the most lavish residence in the Rue de Varenne . . . or the Avenue du Bois. But he acquired an old house overlooking the Seine, with plain plastered façades pierced by regular rows of uniform windows; one of those timeless houses in which Paris is so rich and which offer a perfect example of 'standard' accommodation; that is, the standard of the pre-machine age, which goes back to the time of Henry IV. Mr M— set up home there with limewashed walls.

distances have been shortened; the manager of a factory can now shake hands with the gate-keeper. Voisin, who wants to win the Grand Prix, depends on his driver Rougier, and urges him on; Rougier is dependent on his mechanic, and he urges *him* on; Voisin also urges on his mechanic, until not even the apprentice is left out of the party.

Gilding is fading out and the slums will not be with us long before they are abolished.

There is no longer such a thing as a private palace; luxury no longer resides in the Aubusson carpet but has moved up to the brain. Working-class housing can already provide bright and healthy spaces, and the word bathroom is entering everyday speech. There is no more than four sous between the price of a first class and a second class ticket on the Metro; the platform of a bus is a democratic spot where the men in flat caps and the gentlemen in raglans pile in together; inclining his cap, the man says with confidence: 'Got a light please, mister?'

The life of the great machine age has profoundly stirred up society, has cut through all locks, has thrown open all doors, has cast its glance everywhere; today the rich know what poverty is, because they can see it unvarnished; the poor have a fair idea what wealth is, because they can assess it directly or indirectly, through contact or in the cinema.

I say this not to 'shoot a line', but to direct attention for one minute to this revolution. For the 1925 Exhibition of *Decorative Art* (since we *must* call it by its name!) will force it on our attention and will perhaps give us new eyes – those whom idleness has turned into pillars of salt, their faces turned back towards 'things as they always were'.

Certainly, we appear to be working towards the establishment of a simple and economical *human scale*. Simplicity grows out of complexity; economy from richness. This last millennium since the Barbarians has worked hard, and has enjoyed the boisterous pleasures of adolescence. When my aunt gave me twenty sous, I ran off to buy cakes covered with cream and icing sugar, masterpieces of craftsmanship, pagodas! I thought myself a prince. But today we seem to realise that however rich we are, we cannot eat a whole chicken each. The chicken fixes the key to the human scale. The whole oxen that were once roasted at ancestral banquets now fill no more than the centre of a dinner-plate: the beef steak. We are tending to rediscover the human scale; and in the world of appearance and consumption, of thought and of deed, of joy in the heart and gesture in the hands, to rediscover the human scale is to approach wisdom. Diogenes is not so far away.

If the hard life of this machine age makes us bitter that is because a page has been turned; we have a new existence, one which is not so very playful.

The dance-halls? the theatres, nudity in the music hall? These reflect

Farman-Goliath fuselage.
Enormous strength, astonishing lightness, slenderness and breadth.

legitimate needs – purgative needs. Purgative, because we are waiting for this completely new society to organise itself. The march of progress is an imperious goddess, neither good nor bad, neutral, quite simply blind; she has a whip which spares no one. To struggle against it would be to break one's back; either it is to be very rich to be able to (in which case one breaks the back of one's pleasure), or else it is to become the 'non-conforming artist' and to be unemployed (in which case one breaks the back of one's dignity).

Not to struggle against it but to participate with joy in this magnificent current is to direct one's life, stretched by labour, to creative ends – a life which is due its rest through recreation of the body and its crowning joy through the speculations of the mind.

Such a life promises to be more demanding. But progress, which is its driving force, also gives us the means to stimulate the inner life (the first of these means was the book).

To the rich man, his father said: 'You have suppressed everything that money can provide.' This American businessman was expressing a simple thought. But voiced by a child of our age, it was the high moral principle of our age, to which his spirit was obscurely aspiring.

The consequences of the crisis which has divided pre-machine society from the new machine-age society are already upon us and are continuing to develop; in our innermost thoughts we are no more than beginning to perceive them.

***

Here, without comment, is the little song of a cabin-boy sitting astride the masthead of a ship that is going to be torpedoed this fine autumn afternoon.

PARIS,ce 26 Mars 1922.

LITTÉRATURE
A R T S
ÉLÉGANCE⌇

Monsieur,

"FLIRT"!évoque en une seule et unique syllabe tout le
charme des heures délicieuses de notre vie moderne...

"FLIRT",dont le premier numéro paraître le 15 mai pro-
chain, n'est pas une nouvelle Revue quelconque,c'est,
rénové selon le goût du jour, l'ensemble des tendances
qui ont fait du XVIII° siècle,celui entre tous le plus
représentatif de notre caractère national,en ce qu'il
a de plus vaporeux,de plus fin,de plus brillant.......

"FLIRT"c'est le champagne qui mousse,pétille...C'est
l'esprit frondeur de Voltaire,le madrigal de Marivaux,
la grâce de Boucher,de Watteau,de Fragonard..........

and so it goes on!*

*See note on p. 48 for translation. J.I.D.

Structural testing of a fuselage. This can resist storms, and has an enormous cantilever!

* * *

So the 1925 Exhibition of Decorative Art (since we have to call it by its name) forces our attention on this silent revolution which is taking place all around us and inside us, and as a result of which we no longer behave like our grandparents.

To behave, that is, to move about, to pick up things, to handle things, to look and to see.

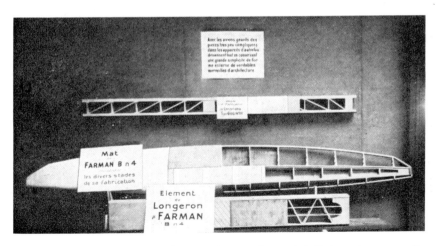

Spars and struts of an aeroplane. These are elements that work to their maximum capacity and are as light as a bird. Rich in strength and economical in material. Opulent outline and delicate profiles that are quite *certain*, and lead us to those of the Parthenon.

The way we look is different, what we see and the way we see it are also different.

The task of the decorative arts (who will think of a better name?) is above all to make us feel comfortable, by serving us politely and helpfully. After that, it is to thrill us, let there be no mistake.

* * *

So it is first of all a question of organisation, of internal mechanism. Do you not feel that certain industries normally excluded from the decorative arts are already tackling these questions? And that if this task was clear, industry, so obliging, so ingenious, so zealous, so intoxicating in its attentions,[1] would come running to help? Yes, let us admit it. And to illustrate the sort of consequences one could expect, let us pause before one example, that of construction in timber, which is fundamental to furniture, and as a result to the decorative arts as a whole. First of all, we assert without ambiguity

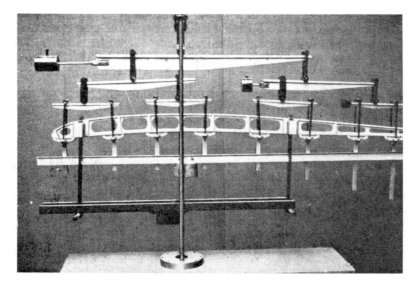

Testing the ribs of aeroplanes. Economy takes wood in the same direction as metal: steel sections, the girders of bridges, etc.

1. The banker who pulls the lever of his calculator, the writer who soliloquizes into the mouthpiece of his dictaphone.

Fabrication of a monocoque fuselage. And calculation and economy are accused of leading to meanness! In fact, here is a new craft for which we are unprepared, unequipped.

that there is no reason why wood should continue to be the essential raw material for the furniture manufacturer. If asked, industry will immediately propose new helpmates: steel, aluminium, cement (of a particular specification), fibre, and . . . the unknown! . . . The Faubourg Saint-Antoine will then send its apprentices to Levalloise, to Issy-les-Moulineaux, to the aircraft factories and car factories. (Heaven forbid that this last suggestion should be turned by ubiquitous journalism into the latest sensation, a cliché, a fad, the catch-phrase of tomorrow!) The aircraft factory and the coachworks use wood in such new ways that furniture of wood no longer has the right to be thought of in the same way as before, and you and me, who 'think furniture' with our traditional baggage, well, we are no longer good for anything: we have to re-educate ourselves. On one side lies the economics of the past, and on the other, that of the present; it is founded on a major science, on experimentation (often dramatic: aircraft), on the work of laboratories.

The age is new, with its inescapable consequences; the vitality of the country and the life-giving fact of progress demand that we look to its implications. It is this that must be demonstrated. The principle applies everywhere.

To continue to sow fruitful doubt, let us suggest a few games of consequences:

Electricity and candles?

Glass from Saint-Gobain and wooden windows with little panes and coloured glass?

Rolled steel sections and wrought iron?

The joyful light of day and embroidered hangings?

The dining-car (room for eighty diners) and elaborate place-settings in the style of Louis XVI?

The eight-hour day for domestic servants and our boudoir-bazaars full of trinkets?

The crisis in transport, the cost of trucking, and those lovely thick walls which make such beautiful window reveals?

Fine porcelain and local pottery?

Central heating and thick old logs that spark?

The decorative arts and the 1925 Exhibition draw our attention to this silent revolution in our tools, that is blind but changes everything.

*_**

To thrill us henceforth, the decorative arts *will heed* the Diogenean sentiment: 'You have suppressed everything that money can provide.'

Let us keep to the spirit, and not quibble about the letter!

PARIS, 26 March 1922   FLIRT

LITERATURE ARTS FASHION

Dear Sir,

'FLIRT'! evokes in a single and unique syllable all the charm of the golden hours of our modern life . . .

'FLIRT', whose first number will appear on 15 May, is not just another new magazine, it is the synthesis – brought up to date with the taste of today – of all the styles and ideas which made the eighteenth century the most representative of our national character in all that is lightest, finest, and most brilliant . . .

'FLIRT' is the champagne that bubbles, that sparkles . . . It is the critical spirit of Voltaire, the madrigal of Marivaux, the grace of Boucher, of Watteau, of Fragonard . . .

1925

EXPO.

ARTS. DÉCO.

5

One day the railway engine succeeded in setting the whole world in motion.

It was the age of metal, the steel age. *The steel in our hands was the machine; with the machine came calculation; with calculation, the solution of a hypothesis; with the solution of a hypothesis, the resolution of a dream. In the space of a hundred years, revolution was fomented: the industrial revolution, the social revolution, the moral revolution.*

Industry blew upon the world, and there was a hurricane.

The industrialist thought to himself: 'let us smother our junk with decoration: decoration hides all manner of flaws and blemishes.' Camouflage is sanctified. Desperate inspiration and commercial triumph.

N° 78-402. **LA SALAMANDRE** che
minee roulante feu visible et continu
forme carrée Louis xv et Louis xvi
Fonte brute **420.** » ornements
nickelés **525.**» Email majol **580.**»

A HURRICANE

The whole business had been brewing for some time; but it burst upon the
world suddenly. Stephenson had set some comical engines on some rudi-
mentary rails; then one day they succeeded in setting the whole world in
motion. It was now the age of metal, a new iron age, in fact *the steel age*. The
steel in our hands became the machine: with the machine came calculation;
with calculation, the solution of a hypothesis; with the solution of a hypothesis, the resolution of a dream. In the space of a hundred years, revolution
was fomented: the industrial revolution, the social revolution, the moral
revolution. This is what has happened, or is happening. Industry blew upon

the world, and there was a hurricane. If the vital axes of social organisation became misaligned, imagine the microcosm of confusion in the heart of the individual: the hurricane overturned on us without restraint the miraculous fruits of the first industrial age; these came in the form of a cornucopia carved with gadroons and acanthus leaves, in the manner of the craftsmen of the KINGS – baubles catalogued by archaeologists born precisely in this disjointed era. No one had any idea what the real outcome of the adventure would be.

M. LOUIS-PHILIPPE, with his whiskers, said simply to himself: 'This will allow me to bring some glitter into my little home, on the cheap.' And so it did.

THE BOURGEOIS SAID: 'It's astonishing; I'm gathering the fruit ripened by the Revolution: we have cut off the head of Capet; now I'm king, long live the king!

I would like to have my stove decorated with leaf ornament (Benvenuto Cellini) cubic value: BC^3;

My windows hung with lace curtains (Valenciennes, Venice, Bruges, Scotland) combined according to the formula: $A_m^n = m(m - 1)(m - 2) \ldots (m - n + 1)$;

15.295. COUVRE-LIT guipure filet
imitation dentelle, teinte crème
franges tout autour.
Dimensions 2ᵐ50 × 2ᵐ30
35.50

My Louis XIV armchairs (so majestic) with an admixture of Louis XVI (of such distinction): $(a + b)^2 = a^2 + b^2 + 2ab$;

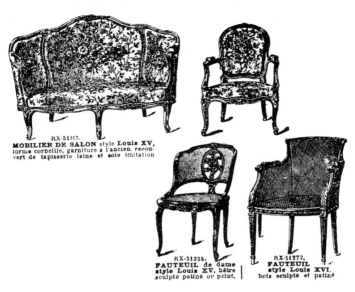

RX-51317.
MOBILIER DE SALON style **Louis XV,**
forme corbeille, garniture à l'ancien, recouvert de tapisserie laine et soie imitation

RX-51325.
FAUTEUIL de dame
style Louis XV, hêtre
sculpté patiné ou peint,

RX-51272.
FAUTEUIL
style Louis XVI,
bois sculpté et patiné

My walls papered with damask, *Compagnie des Indes*, Genoa, Venice – arithmetic progression: $S = na + \dfrac{n(n - 1)}{2} r$;

MB-50660. **MOBILIER** de chambre à concher style Louis XVI, acajou marqueterie et bronze, ciré rempli, très belle fabrication. Comprenant : 1 armoire. *Hauteur* 1m40

My panelling like the Galerie des Glaces, in imitation marble, etc.'

OI-34756 'Amour Musicien'. GARNITURE bronze
Imitation, socle marbre, mouvement garanti, à sonnerie
et quinzaine.

OI-34807. COLONNE marbre
vert de mer ou rouge royal,
monture bronze, décoré ton

II-34790. " LION AUX AGUETS "
Sujet vrai bronze. Long. 0◦45.

(But at the same time, the railway engines, commerce, calculation, the struggle for precision, put his frills in question, and his clothing tended to become a plain black, or mottled; the bowler hat appeared on the horizon. Darwin's law was applied with swifter fatality to this living individual than to his accessories.)

THE INDUSTRIALIST SAID (he was faced for the first time with the problem of exactitude and his products were prone to last minute hitches): 'Quite clearly, for an acceptable price I can only produce junk. But decoration will save me; let us cover *everything* with decoration. Let us hide the junk beneath decoration; decoration hides flaws, blemishes, all defects.' Desperate inspiration and commercial triumph.

Decoration on all castings (iron, copper, bronze, tin, etc.).
Decoration on all fabrics (curtains, furnishings, fashions).
Decoration on all white linen (table clothes, underwear, bed linen).
Decoration on all papers.
Decoration on all pottery and porcelain.
Decoration on all glassware.

Decoration in all departments! Decoration, decoration: yes indeed, in all departments; the department store became the 'ladies' joy'!

MB-50219 **BUFFET** Renaissance, noyer ciré sculpté

TA-28690.**TASSES** "Liverdy" porcelaine de Limoges, marque Lantornier, décor guirlande de bleuets, bord jaspé or.
La tasse à café. **6.25**
La tasse à thé. **6.75**
La tasse à déjeûner **10.50**

TA-28683. **HUILIER** faïence, très joli décor genre ancien **19**

TA-28690. **SAUCIÈRE** fruit maigre, porcelaine décor bordure. **9.75**

TA 28644. **SERVICE** "MALLET", porcelaine, décor moderne, jetés de fleurs.

NF-62321 **SERVICE**, Empire, orfèvrerie mas-

NF-62316 **SERVICE** Louis XVI, orfèvrerie massive argentée, modèle riche, anses palissandre et métal.

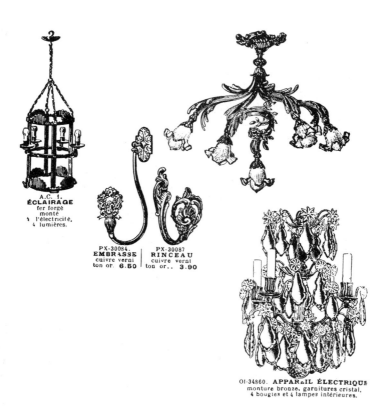

A.C. 1.
ÉCLAIRAGE
fer forgé
monté
à l'électricité,
4 lumières.

PX-30084.
EMBRASSE
cuivre verni
ton or. **6.50**

PX-30087
RINCEAU
cuivre verni
ton or.. **3.90**

OI-34860. **APPAREIL ÉLECTRIQUE**
monture bronze, garnitures cristal,
4 bougies et 4 lampes intérieures.

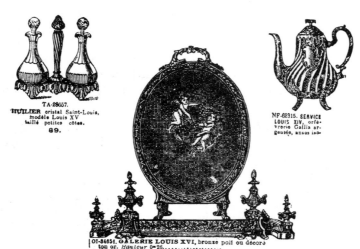

TA-28657.
HUILIER cristal Saint-Louis,
modèle Louis XV
taillé petites côtes.
89.

NF-62315. **SERVICE
LOUIS XIV**, orfè-
vrerie Gallia ar-
gentée, anses iso-

OI-34651. **GALERIE LOUIS XVI**, bronze poli ou décoré
ton or. *Hauteur* 0m26........................

Even the most wishful decree would not be able to abrogate such a commercial postulate.

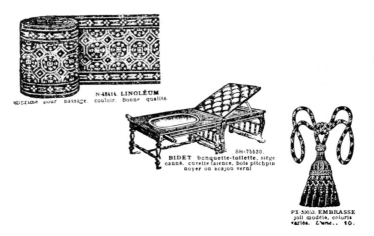

N-48414. LINOLÉUM
imprime pour passage. couloir. Bonne qualité.

SH-75530.
BIDET banquette-toilette, siège canné, cuvette faience, bois pitchpin noyer ou acajou verni

PX-30053. EMBRASSE
joli modèle, coloris variés. L'une., 10.

THE PEASANT ON THE DANUBE CHOSE:

He chose decoration, because it was at the heart of his peasant's soul. He said: 'my everyday crockery, my everyday clothes, are uniform, plain, and grey.' The railway brought him wagon-loads full of delicate porcelain covered with roses as fine as the flowers themselves, with seashells, and leafy tendrils of the brightest gold. The peasant on the Danube was immediately dazzled, quite overcome, and lost faith in his folk culture: he let it drop like a load of bricks, wherever the railways reached – throughout the world . . .

Even the Last of the Mohicans! It was only in the aristocratic houses of the big cities that committees were formed to save the folk cultures; conferences, lectures, magazines, exhibitions. Later, the cinema would finish off the work of the railways. The peasant on the Danube has chosen. Folk culture no longer exists, only ornament on mass-produced junk. Everywhere!

PX-30075.
TAPIS DE TABLE
imitation tapisserie.
dessin médaillon
sur fond rouge ou vert.
encadre et frangé.

MB-50495. GLACE
encadrement bronze
rehaussé d'or,
joli profil.

La fraicheur fait environ 0ᵐ14.

Hₜ. ext. fraîchea aux compris.	La même sans fraises
80X 59.	135. 120.
89X 62.	150. 135.
101X 68.	195. 175.
107X 77.	235. 210.
116X 83.	285. 260.
128X 92.	340. 315.
137X 98.	450. 375.

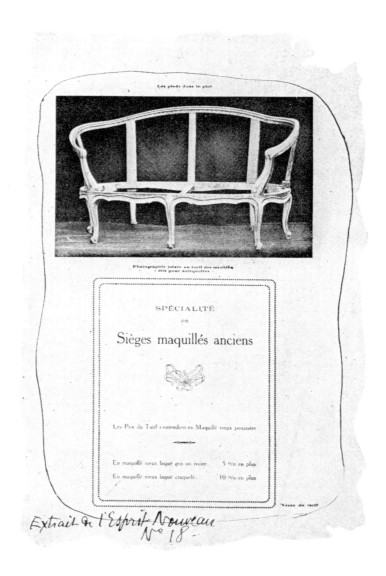

Authentic confidential documents relating to the fabrication of false
antiques, supposedly for 'lovers of the antique'.

TARIF 1923

Le présent Tarif annule tout précédent

SIÈGES MAQUILLÉS VIEUX POUSSIÈRE

N°	Désignation	Prix	N°	Désignation	Prix	N°	Désignation	Prix
322	Chaise	210.—	531 B	Caqueteuse	285.—	623	Fauteuil	225.—
337	Fauteuil	275.—	540	Bergère haute	275.—	624	Bergère	390.—
365	"	255.—	540	Bergère basse	275.—	625	Lit repos	515.—
371	"	145.—	545	Caqueteuse	270.—	626	Fauteuil	275.—
377	Caqueteuse	270.—	549	Chaise	135.—	629	Chaise	165.—
378	Chaise	85.—	561	Chaise	165.—	630	Rauteuil	230.—
"	Cannée	145.—	562	Fauteuil	270.—	637	Fauteuil	310.—
"	Fauteuil	175.—	564	Fauteuil	265.—	640	Fauteuil	315.—
"	Canapé	255.—	566	Bergère	235.—	641	Fauteuil	245.—
486	Fauteuil	190.—	567	Fauteuil	245.—	642	Fauteuil	245.—
487	"	245.—	568	Bergère	240.—	643	Fauteuil	225.—
488	"	200.—	569	Fauteuil	225.—	644	Fauteuil	295.—
489	"	225.—	570	Chaise	115.—	645	Fauteuil	295.—
498	"	190.—	571	Fauteuil	255.—	646	Bergère	485.—
499	"	225.—	572	Canapé	375.—	648	Bergère	285.—
500	Bergère	235.—	573	Marquise	260.—	649	Fauteuil	210.—
502	Lit repos	525.—	574	Chaise	125.—	650	Canapé	335.—
504	Canapé	525.—	585	Fauteuil	285.—	"	Fauteuil	225.—
"	Le Fauteuil	265.—	591	Lit repos	565.—	"	Chaise	125.—
505	Canapé	525.—	592	Fauteuil	235.—	"	Bergère	245.—
506	Bergère	285.—	594	Bergère	255.—	"	Lit repos	680.—
508	"	235.—	595	Fauteuil	225.—	658	Bergère	295.—
510	Fauteuil	225.—	599	Lit repos	480.—	662	Chaise	95.—
512	"	335.—	601	Canapé	345.—	663	Fauteuil	310.—
514	Chaise	145.—	602	Chaise-longue	315.—	664	"	205.—
517	"	175.—	604	Fauteuil	295.—	666	"	295.—
520	Lit repos	525.—	605	Fauteuil	225.—	667	Banquette	185.—
521	Fauteuil	190.—	614	Canapé	375.—	668	Banquette	185.—
522	Bergère	235.—	614	Bergère	260.—	669	Bergère	325.—
525	Chaise longue	490.—	616	Madone 35 cm.	135.—	672	Lit repos	580.—
526	Canapé	305.—	616	Madone 48 cm.	175.—	673	Fauteuil	235.—
528	Chaise	125.—	620	Fauteuil	255.—	674	"	245.—
530	Fauteuil	215.—	621	Chaise-longue	555.—	675	"	235.—
531	Fauteuil	195.—	622	Bergère	260.—	677	"	270.—

Extract from *L'Esprit Nouveau*, No. 18. Authentic confidential documents relating to the fabrication of false antiques, supposedly for 'lovers of the antique'.

Photograph attached to the price list of 'antique' furniture.

Spécialité de Sieges
maquillés ancien

Nos sièges " dits pour antiquaires „
s'entendent : Construction à l'ancienne, vieux bois
chevillés, Assemblages verticaux, Mortaises,
traces de clous aux feuillures, Patine ancienne, etc...

La plupart de nos sièges sont copiés d'après
des modèles anciens

'. . . our chairs for "lovers of the antique" have these features: antique methods of construction, old pinned wood, vertical jointing, mortices, nail holes in the rebates, antique patina, etc . . .' Extract from the prospectus of a fabricator.

*
* *

Heartbreaking.

Heartbroken, *THE GOOD ART-LOVER SAID*: We must return to nature. Nature is beautiful because it is *sentient*. And the conclusion, by way of an impeccable syllogism, is: 'nature' means making things by hand, because the hand is sentient, and what is more, it is natural.

To make everything by hand: faced by the inexhaustible products of industry, the products of the machine, this was the slogan: *handicraft*. Mystique. Evocation of Bernard Palissy.* Invention of running glazes. The gamble of the firing, that's nature; the running glaze that fails, that's nature: the cult of 'failures'.

*French sixteenth-century ceramicist who made extensive use of ornament in high relief on his wares. J.I.D.

THE MINISTERS OF CULTURE, THE POLITICAL LEADERS SAID: 'Craftsmanship must be saved.' The press could ask for nothing better than to make copy out of this theme:

EXHIBITION OF CRAFT-WORK

The craftsman! Will this class of free workman, who one imagined had disappeared in the revolutionary tide, experience a revival in our midst? Modern machinery would certainly seem to make his existence impossible, and so in fact it has proved in most sectors of industry, where at a time of rising costs mass-production is more and more the rule.
. . . .

Interesting evidence is offered on this question by the national exhibition of crafts which has just opened at the Grand Palais. There are unusual examples of craftsmanship on show, many of which have real artistic quality; they prove that handicraft, the glory of our parents, has survived the numerous assaults of a society obsessed with speed. Even better: there are signs of a magnificent renaissance.

On one side there are works in wrought iron which the craftsman has fashioned and worked as he pleased, sometimes giving it the shape of a flower, sometimes rivalling lace in grace and fantasy. On the other, there is glassware, porcelain, and stoneware decorated by hand. Elsewhere, there are fabrics decorated with stencilled ornament, etc.
. . . .

In sum, this exhibition is full of success already achieved, and of happy promise. We sincerely congratulate the organisers as much as the exhibitors. And we hope, in conclusion, that the authorities will not rest content with having afforded craft-work the necessary credit facilities, but will allow them by the establishment of Chambers for the Crafts, to develop, and enhance the reputation of French Art.

(Les Débats. 17 July 1924)

The editors of art magazines encouraged 'this thing' and the publishers got to work.

YOUNG PEOPLE SAY TO THEMSELVES (for one cannot help knowing that henceforth the machine has decreed inflexible precision and pitiless rigour): 'Handicraft. Cult of "failures". Excuse for daubs. Slack hour of imprecision. Triumph of weak egoism. Delight of the free will, regard for the individual. Refusal of control.

Refusal of control. Liberty.

Oh Liberty!

Here then is the field where liberty still reigns. The outstanding refuge for liberty, which everywhere else is stamped on and repressed . . .'

THE PUBLIC MARCHED: Yes, the public marched, and is marching. Magnificently.

– Really?

– Keep quiet, here comes the International Exhibition of 1925.

Silence! Stirring sounds are reported in the distance.

A fortune-teller: '1926? The Hurricane has passed!'

The Meteorological Office, Mr Nordman: 'Ditto.'

* *
*

Elsewhere, in the clear light of day, the mechanic has founded a new order by his accomplishment.

    The stone age.
    The bronze age.
    The iron age.
. . . .

Today: *the steel age.*

The door to the strong-room of a bank.

Note 1.   The illustrations in this chapter certainly convulse one with laughter! But these ornaments – this style, in a word – were taken directly from works of the past considered excellent.
        So how will the modern decorative arts fare in fifty, or even twenty years time? When we
see the pictures in the catalogues that flood the whole country, Paris, the regions, and abroad,
and there form the taste of the masses, we say: the art of the concierge!
        What will be the judgement of our children on the work of the numerous decorators who
have given up the styles and are applying themselves to 'modern' decoration?
Note 2.   All the objects illustrated in this chapter are currently on sale in shops in Paris.

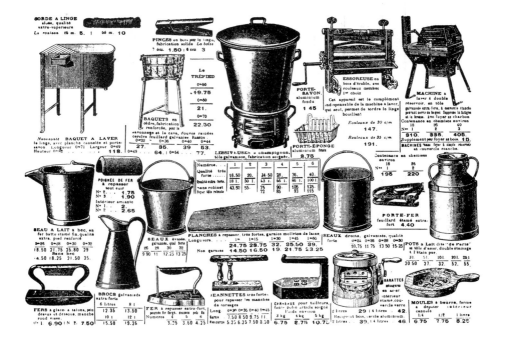

1925

EXPO,
ARTS. DÉCO.

6

To search for human scale, for human function, is to define human needs.
These needs are 'type'. We all need means of supplementing our natural capabilities.
Human-limb objects *are type-objects responding to type-needs.*
Decorative art is an inexact and wordy phrase by which we denote the totality of human-limb objects. *These respond with some precision to certain clearly established needs. Type-needs, type-functions, therefore type-objects and type-furniture.*
The human-limb object is a docile servant. A good servant is discreet and self-effacing, in order to leave his master free.
Works of decorative art are tools, beautiful tools.

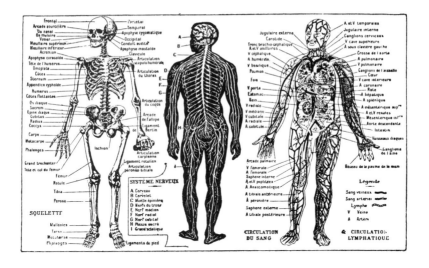

TYPE-NEEDS
TYPE-FURNITURE

Here we quit the anguished realms of fantasy and the incongruous, and resume a code with reassuring articles. The poet goes into decline, it's true; he chucks up cornices and baldacchinos and makes himself more useful as a cutter in a tailor's shop, with a man standing in front of him and he, metre in hand, taking measurements. Here we are back on *terra firma*. The uplifting calm of certainty!

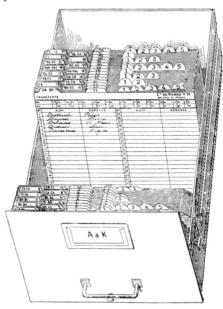

'Roneo' files.

When one factor in our technico-cerebro-emotional equation grows disproportionately, a crisis occurs, since the relationships are disturbed – the relationships between our cerebro-emotional being and the things we use

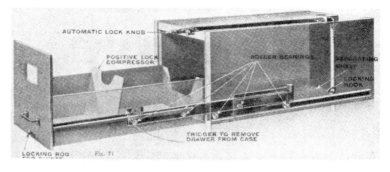

The drawers run smoothly on rollers.

that are around us: we continue to make them as before, or else we anticipate or react against recognized reality. The feeling for cause and effect falters. We are seized by disquiet because we no longer feel well adapted; we revolt against our enforced servitude to the *abnormal*, whether it is retrogressive or too far ahead of its time.

The compass will save us from this disturbance; the compass in this case is ourselves: a man, a constant, the fixed point that in truth is the only object of our concern. We must therefore always seek to rediscover the *human scale*, the human function.

Since the crisis has now come to a head, there is no more urgent task than to force ourselves to re-adjust to our functions, in all fields. To free our

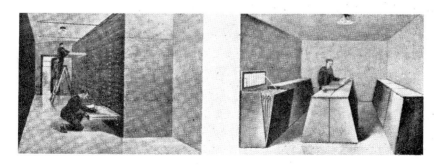

How drawings can be filed better
(Roneo).
The search for improvement leads to quite new ideas.

attention for a few moments from bondage to its habitual tasks and to think about *the why*, reflect, weigh up, decide. And to answer *the why* with innocence, simplicity, and candour. This is as much as to say, to set aside our acquired preconceptions, to deposit our fund of memories in the safe of our bank in the third basement, behind a steel door, and leaving alongside it the whole poetic of the past, to formulate our most fundamental desires.

To search for the human scale, for human function, is to define human needs.

They are not very numerous; they are very similar for all mankind, since man has been made out of the same mould from the earliest times known to us. Faced with the task of providing a definition of man, Larousse calls on just three images to portray his anatomy; the whole machine is there, the structure, the nervous system, the arterial system, and this applies to every single one of us exactly and without exception.

These needs are type, that is to say they are the same for all of us; *we all need means of supplementing our natural capabilities*, since nature is indifferent, inhuman (extra-human), and inclement; we are born naked and with insufficient armour. Thus the cupped hands of Narcissus led us to invent the bottle; the barrel of Diogenes, already a notable improvement on our natural protective organs (our skin and scalp), gave us the primordial cell of the house; filing cabinets and copy-letters make good the inadequacies of our memory; wardrobes and sideboards are the containers in which we put away the auxiliary limbs that guarantee us against cold or heat, hunger or thirst, etc. These apparently paradoxical definitions take us far from Decorative Art; they are the very reason for this chapter.

In speaking of decorative art, we have the right to insist on the type-quality of our needs, since our concern is with the mechanical system that surrounds us, which is no more than an extension of our limbs; its elements, in fact, *artificial limbs*. Decorative art becomes orthopaedic, an activity that appeals to the imagination, to invention, to skill, but a craft analogous to the tailor: the client is a man, familiar to us all and precisely defined.

This view is shared by the designers of car bodywork, the furnishers of cinemas, the manufacturers of glassware and crockery, even by the architects who design apartments to let. Nevertheless, one of the big names in charge of the 1925 Exhibition recently disagreed violently; with his heart set on multifold poetry, he proclaimed the need of each individual for something different, claiming different circumstances in each case: the fat man, the thin man, the short, the long, the ruddy, the lymphatic, the violent, the mild, the utopian, and the neurasthenic; then the vocations: the dentist, and the man of letters, the architect and the merchant, the navigator and the astronomer, etc. He sees the character of an individual as dictating his every act, and by an elliptical process of reasoning, as shaping his tools – tools that will be particular, individual, and unique to him, and have nothing in common with those of his neighbour. *Life, that's life, I believe in nothing but life. You are killing the individual!* Thus a fabulous, uncountable field of activity for the orthopaedist, a field whose limitless immensity makes one dizzy.

Would this then be, at last, miraculously, *the much sought after definition of the term*: DECORATIVE ART? To the *tool-object*, the *human-limb object*, is now opposed the *sentiment-object*, the *life-object*.

The argument would hold, since at the last count it is indisputable that only *poetry*, that is to say, happiness, carries authority. But first let us recognise the practical impossibility of this dream of an individual *sentiment-object*, in all its infinite multiplicity; let us observe that our interlocutor in fact has in mind an *objet d'art*, and we will reply to that later. And so, since happiness is our objective, let us propose an alternative definition of happiness: happiness lies in the creative faculty, in the most elevated possible activity. Life (and the cost of living!) subjects us to labour (labour that is generally imposed, and therefore scarcely creative) and for a great many people their hour of happiness is very far from the hours spent earning their bread. An elevated activity: to manage, by means of those stimulants which for us are the achievements of life – that is, music, books, the creations of the spirit – to lead a life that is truly one's own, truly oneself. That means a life

Composition based on standards leading to mechanical perfection (Roneo).

Furniture of steel sheet leads to the perfection of the mechanical (Roneo).

that is *individual*; and thus *the individual is placed on the highest level, the only level*, but detached from the secondary level of his tools. These activities of the spirit, this introspection, which can delve only a little way, or very deeply, is life itself, that is, one's internal life, one's true life. So in no sense has life been killed, thank God! And neither has the individual!

Sentiment-objects or *objets d'art* are nothing but dross in comparison with this inner fire – slight charm and certain encumbrance, most likely trifles, clowns, jesters – intended merely for distraction (I am speaking here of decorative *objets d'art*). The legitimate *sentiment-object* lies far off and higher up, in a purified abode on a more elevated plane; then it is a *work of art*, and as such it is another matter altogether. For we may certainly believe in a hierarchy, and not put a piece of poker-work on the same level as the *Sistine Chapel* (nor glass beads, embroidery, or ornamental woodwork). But we will return to that later, and rest content for the time being with this initial classification.

For our comfort, to facilitate our work, to avoid exhaustion, to refresh ourselves, in one word to *free our spirit* and distance us from the clutter that encumbers our life and threatens to *kill it*, we have equipped ourselves

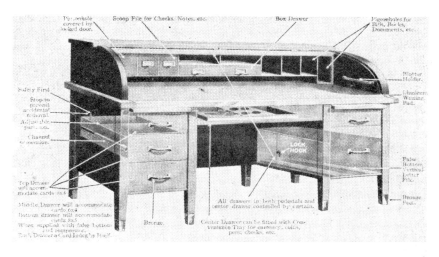

Steel furniture (Roneo).

through our ingenuity with *human-limb objects*, extensions of our limbs; and by making use of these tools, we avoid unpleasant tasks, accidents, the sterile drudgery which according to our interlocutor constitutes precisely the richness and multiplicity of life; we *organise our affairs* and, having won our freedom, we think about something – about art for example (for it is very comforting).

The *human-limb objects* are type-objects, responding to type-needs: chairs to sit on, tables to work at, devices to give light, machines to write with (yes indeed!), racks to file things in.

This is cold and brutal, but it's right and true; the basis is there (Ormo).

If our spirits vary, our skeletons are alike, our muscles are in the same places and perform the same functions: dimensions and mechanism are thus fixed. So the problem is posed and the question is: who will solve it ingeniously, reliably, and cheaply? Since we are sensitive to the harmony that brings repose, we recognise an object that is in harmony with our limbs. When a and b are equal to c, a and b are equal to each other. In this case, $a = $ our *human-limb objects*; $b = $ our sense of harmony; $c = $ our body. Thus *human-limb objects* are in accord with our sense of harmony in that they are in accord with our bodies.[1] So we are satisfied . . . *until the next development in these tools.*

We have now identified decorative art as commensurate with the art of the engineer. The art of the engineer extends across a wide spectrum of human activity. If at one extreme it encompasses pure calculation and mechanical invention, at the other it leads towards *Architecture*.

Can one then speak of the architecture of decorative art, and consider it capable of permanent value?

The permanent value of decorative art? Let us say more exactly, of the *objects* that surround us. This is where we exercise our judgement: first of all the Sistine Chapel, afterwards chairs and filing cabinets; without doubt this is a question of the secondary level, just as the cut of a man's jacket is of secondary importance in his life. Hierarchy. First of all the Sistine Chapel, that is to say works truly etched with passion. Afterwards machines for sitting in, for filing, for lighting, type-machines, the problem of purification, of simplification, of precision, before the problem of poetry.[2]

---

1. When the typewriter came into use, letter paper was standardised; this standardisation had considerable repercussions upon furniture as a result of the establishment of a module, that of the *commercial format*. Typewriters, file-copies, filing trays, files, filing drawers, filing cabinets, in a word the whole furnishing industry, was affected by the establishment of this standard; and even the most intransigent individualists were not able to resist it. An international convention was established. These questions are of such importance that international commissions meet regularly to establish the standards. The *commercial format* is not an arbitrary measure. Rather, let us appreciate the wisdom (the anthropocentric mean) that established it. In all things that are in universal use, individual fantasy bows before human fact. Here are some figures: the ratio of vertical to horizontal dimension in the commercial format is 1·3. That of a sheet of Ingres paper is 1·29. That of the sectors of the plans of Paris established by Napoleon I is 1·33; that of the Taride plans 1·33. That of most magazines 1·28. That of canvases for figure painting (time-honoured sizes) is 1·30. That of daily newspapers from 1·3 to 1·45. That of photographic plates 1·5; that of books 1·4 to 1·5, that of kitchen tables in the Bazaar de l'Hotel-de-Ville 1·5; etc., etc.

2. Having established this hierarchy – that is, this channelling of our attention only to those things worthy of it – there remains all round us that group of tools which *we call furniture*. During the long and scrupulous process of development in the factory, the Thonet chair gradually takes on its final weight and thickness, and assumes a format that allows good connections; this process of perfecting by almost imperceptible steps is the same as that to which an engine is subjected, whose poetry is to run well – and cheaply. The Maples armchair, which is attuned to our movements and quick to respond to them, assumes an ever more distinctive profile. The stenographer's desk becomes daily more convenient in the battle of the market place. We have

Much has happened since the age of the Great Kings: the human spirit is more at home behind our foreheads than beneath gilt and carved baldacchinos. 'You have suppressed everything that money can provide'; significant words. Gold, lacquer, marble, brocade are caresses which we look for in the garden of caresses: the ballet, the dance-halls, the elegant restaurants where we dine. Caresses of our senses which are perfectly legitimate at the right time and which deserve to be given well.

Eventually we leave, take a few steps in the bracing air, and return home. We pick up a book or a pen. In this mechanical, discreet, silent, attentive comfort, there is a very fine painting on the wall. Or else: our movements take on a new assurance and precision among walls whose proportions make us happy, and whose colours stimulate us.

Decorative art is an inexact and wordy phrase by which we denote the totality of *human-limb objects*. These respond with some precision to certain clearly established needs. They are extensions of our limbs and are adapted

seen the 'American desk', which seemed to have achieved definitive form, make an about-turn because its development showed up a flaw in its conception. We have learnt that in the context of the rigorous order demanded by business, *it is necessary to have a file on the filing system itself*. The businessman appends to himself supporting limbs: his secretary, his accountant, etc. His documents need a precise place according to type; they are put away in a particular drawer, and the game of filing cards allows them to be retrieved immediately; this function has staff assigned to it, and they have their own furniture. The 'American desk' filed things in a disorderly fashion. So now we have the invaluable arrays of precisely detailed filing cabinets. This new system of filing which clarifies our needs, has an effect on the lay-out of rooms, and of buildings. We have only to introduce this method into our apartments and decorative art will meet its destiny: type-furniture and architecture.

 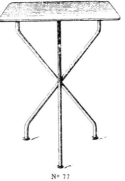

Nº 76
Guéridon rond pliant.
Diametre : 0,50. 0,55, 0,60. 0 70.

Nº 77
Guéridon carre phant.
Côtés : 0 50, 0,55. 0,60.

Roneo.

to human functions that are type-functions. Type-needs, type-functions, therefore type-objects and type-furniture.

The human-limb object is a docile servant. A good servant is discreet and self-effacing, in order to leave his master free.

Certainly, works of decorative art are tools, beautiful tools.

And long live the good taste manifested by choice, suitability, proportion, and harmony!

1925

EXPO.
ARTS. DÉCO.

7

Modern decorative art is not decorated.

But we are told that decoration is necessary to our existence. Let us correct that: art is necessary to us, that is to say, a disinterested passion that exalts us.

So to see things clearly, it is sufficient to separate the satisfaction of disinterested emotion from that of utilitarian need. Utilitarian needs call for tools brought in every respect *to that degree of perfection seen in industry. This then is the great programme for the decorative arts. Day after day industry is turning out tools of perfect utility and convenience that soothe our spirits with the true luxury afforded by the elegance of their conception, the purity of their execution, and the efficiency of their operation.*

This rational perfection and precise formulation in each constitutes sufficient common ground between them to allow the recognition of a style.

THE DECORATIVE ART OF TODAY

The decorative art of today! Am I plunging into paradox? – a paradox that is
only apparent. To include under this rubric everything that is free from

decoration, whilst making due apology for what is simply banal, indifferent, or void of *artistic intention*, to invite the eye and the spirit to take pleasure in the company of such things and perhaps to rebel against the flourish, the stain, the distracting din of colours and ornaments, to dismiss a whole mass of artefacts, some of which are not without merit, to pass over an activity that has sometimes been disinterested, sometimes idealistic, to disdain the work of so many schools, so many masters, so many pupils, and to think thus of them: 'they are as disagreeable as mosquitoes'; and thence to arrive at this impasse: *modern decorative art is not decorated.* Have we not the right? A moment's thought will confirm it. The paradox lies not in reality, but in the words. Why do the objects that concern us here have to be called *decorative art?* This is the paradox: why should chairs, bottles, baskets, shoes, which are all objects of utility, all *tools*, be called *decorative art?* The paradox of making art out of tools. Let's be clear. I mean, the paradox of making *decorative* art out of tools. To make art out of tools is fair enough, if we hold with Larousse's definition, which is that ART is *the application of knowledge to the realisation of an idea.* Then yes. We are indeed committed to apply all our knowledge to the perfect creation of a tool: know-how, skill, efficiency, economy, precision, the sum of knowledge. A good tool, an excellent tool, the very best tool. This is the world of *manufacture*, of industry; we are looking for a standard and our concerns are far from the personal, the arbitrary,

Voison 'Sport'.

Brown-Boveri turbines.

the fantastic, the eccentric; our interest is in the norm, and we are creating type-objects.

So the paradox certainly lies in the terminology.

But we are told that decoration is necessary to our existence. Let us correct that: art is necessary to us; that is to say, a disinterested passion that exalts us. Decoration: baubles, charming entertainment for a savage. (And I do not deny that it is an excellent thing to keep an element of the savage alive in us – a small one.) But in the twentieth century our powers of judgement have developed greatly and we have raised our level of consciousness. Our spiritual needs are different, and higher worlds than those of decoration offer us commensurate experience. It seems justified to affirm: *the more cultivated a people becomes, the more decoration disappears.* (Surely it was Loos who put it so neatly.)

So, to see things clearly, it is sufficient to separate the satisfaction of disinterested emotion from that of utilitarian need. Utilitarian needs call for tools brought in *every respect* to that degree of perfection seen in industry. This then is the magnificent programme for *decorative art* (decidedly, an inappropriate term!).[1]

1. It has to be said that for thirty years no one has been able to find an accurate term. Is that not because the activity lacks precision, lacks direction, and that as a result it is impossible to define it? The Germans invented the word *Kunstgewerb* (industrial art); that is even more equivocal! I was forgetting that pejorative term *applied art*.

To provoke elevated sensations is the prerogative of proportion, which is a sensed mathematic; it is afforded most particularly by architecture,[1] painting, and sculpture – works of no immediate utility, disinterested, exceptional, works that are plastic creations invested with passion, the

Light fitting in the First National Company, Detroit.

passion of a man – the manifold drama that arrests us, jolts us, rouses us, moves us.[2] Now and always there is a hierarchy. There is a time for work, when one uses oneself up, and also a time for meditation, when one recovers one's bearing and rediscovers harmony. There should be no confusion between them; we are no longer in the age of the dilettante, but at an hour that is harsh and epic, serious and violent, pressured and productive, fertile and economic. Everything has its classification; work and meditation.

The classes too have their classification: those who struggle for their crust of bread have the simple ideal of a decent lodging (and they love to see the fanciest furniture, Henry II or Louis XV, which gives them the feeling of

1. Architecture begins where calculation ends.
2. And without doubt furniture can lead us towards architecture, and in place of decoration we shall see the rise of architecture.

wealth – an elementary ideal). And those well-enough endowed to have the ability and the duty to think (and they aspire to the wisdom of Diogenes).

* * *

'La Tortue', Paris.

Previously, decorative objects were rare and costly. Today they are commonplace and cheap. Previously, plain objects were commonplace and cheap; today they are rare and expensive. Previously, decorative objects were items for special display: the plate which the peasant family hung on the wall and the embroidered waistcoat for holidays; grist for the propaganda of princes. Today decorative objects flood the shelves of the Department Stores; they sell cheaply to shop-girls. If they sell cheaply, it is because they are badly made and because decoration hides faults in their manufacture and the poor quality of their materials: decoration is disguise. It pays the manufacturer to employ a decorator to disguise the faults in his products, to conceal the poor quality of their materials and to distract the eye from their blemishes by offering it the spiced morsels of glowing gold-plate and strident symphonies. Trash is always abundantly decorated; the luxury object is well made, neat and clean, pure and healthy, and its bareness reveals the quality of its manufacture. It is to industry that we owe this

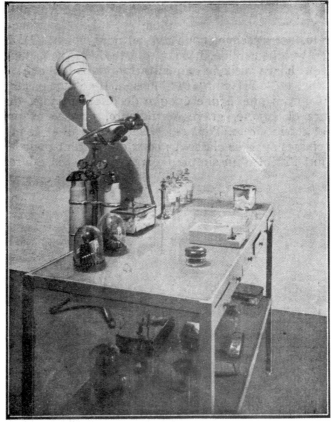

The dentist's surgery of Doctor B.

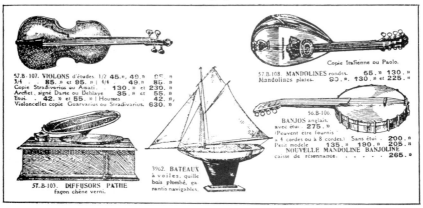

Currently available products.

reversal in the state of affairs: a cast-iron stove overflowing with decoration costs less than a plain one; amidst the surging leaf patterns flaws in the casting cannot be seen. And the same applies generally. Take some plain calico and soak it in colour; the printing machine will instantly cover it in the most fashionable patterns (for example, copies of Spanish mantillas, Bulgarian embroidery, Persian silks, etc.) and without incurring much expense one can

City-National Bank of Tuscaloosa, USA.

double the sale price. I quite agree that it can be as charming, as gay, and as shop-girl-like as you could want, and I would want that to continue. What would spring be without it! But this surface elaboration, if extended without discernment over absolutely everything, becomes repugnant and scandalous; it smells of pretence, and the healthy gaiety of the shop-girl in her flower-patterned cretonne dress, becomes rank corruption when surrounded by Renaissance stoves, Turkish smoking tables, Japanese umbrellas, chamber pots and bidets from Lunéville or Rouen, Bichara perfumes, bordello lamp-shades, pumpkin cushions, divans spread with gold and silver *lamé*, black velvets flecked like the Grand Turk, rugs with baskets of flowers and kissing doves, linoleum printed with Louis XVI ribbons. The pretty little shepherdess shop-girl in her flowery cretonne dress, as fresh as spring, seems, in a bazaar such as this, like a sickening apparition from the show-cases of the costume department in the ethnographic museum.

Not only is this accumulation of false richness unsavoury, but above all and before all, this taste for decorating everything around one is a false taste, an abominable little perversion. I reverse the painting; the shepherdess shop-girl is in a pretty room, bright and clear, white walls, a good chair – wickerwork or Thonet; table from the *Bazaar de l'Hotel de Ville* (in the

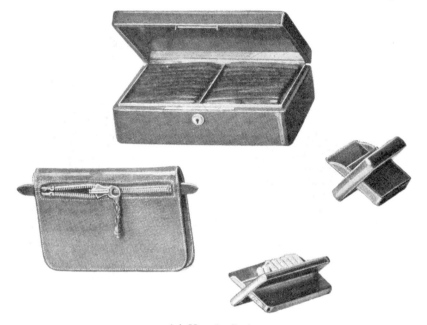

Ad. Hermès, Paris.

manner of Louis XIII, a very beautiful table) painted with ripolin. A good well-polished lamp, some crockery of white porcelain; and on the table three tulips in a vase can be seen lending a lordly presence. It is healthy, clean, decent. And to make something attractive, as little as that is enough.

Certainly, the modern decorative art of the decorators has different objectives, and it is fair to say that the picture I painted above was no more than the vulgarisation of much worthier intentions. So at this point in our search for a guiding principle, we arrive at the impasse of decorative art: decorative art that is not decorated. And we assert that this art without decoration is made not by artists but by anonymous industry following its airy and limpid path of economy.

The guiding principle of decorators with serious intentions is to cater for the enjoyment of life by a sophisticated clientele. As a result of fashions, the publication of books, and the assiduous efforts of a whole generation of decorators, this clientele has seen its tastes sharply awakened to matters connected with art. Today there is a lively aesthetic awareness and a taste for a contemporary art responding to very much more subtle requirements and to a new spirit. As a result there is a distinct evolution towards ideas reflec-

Ad. Hermès, Paris.

ting the new spirit; the experience of decoration as art from 1900 to the war has illustrated the impasse of decoration and the fragility of the attempt to make our tools expressive of sentiment and of individual states of mind. There has been a reaction to this obtrusive presence, and it is being rejected. Day after day, on the other hand, we notice among the products of industry articles of perfect convenience and utility, that soothe our spirits with the luxury afforded by the elegance of their conception, the purity of their execution, and the efficiency of their operation. They are so well thought out that we feel them to be harmonious, and this harmony is sufficient for our gratification.

City-National Bank of Tuscaloosa, USA.

And so, having opened our eyes and rid ourselves of the romantic and Ruskinian baggage that formed our education, we have to ask ourselves whether these new objects do not suit us very well, and whether this rational perfection and precise formulation in each does not constitute sufficient common ground between them to allow the recognition of a *style*!

We have seen that, freed from all reminiscence and traditional pre-conception, a rational and reassuring rigour has been applied to their design. Their choice of material, first of all, has been dictated by considerations of

Saderne, Paris.

City-National Bank of Tuscaloosa, USA.

strength, lightness, economy and durability alone; objects for centuries made of wood have been adapted to metal and steel – objects such as office furniture, from which an entirely new precision of operation is demanded. Thus the 'Voltaire' low armchair has become a totally different machine for sitting in since it was covered in leather.

As a result of this adaptation to new materials, the structure has been transformed, often radically; for a long time these new forms offended us

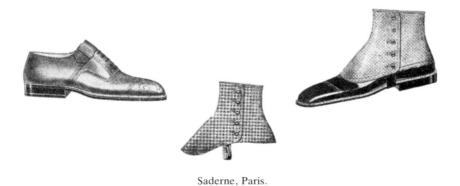

Saderne, Paris.

Commercial glassware and crockery.

and, by a fatal process of reasoning, provoked a violent *nationalist* (that is to say, regionalist) reaction, an appeal to handicraft as opposed to the machine, seen as a modern hydra. A sterile reaction: one cannot swim back against the current, and the machine which does its work with purity and exactitude is from today dispelling this anachronistic backwash. Let us allow one or two generations brought up in the religion of patina and the 'hand-made' to fade away quietly. The young generations are born to the new light

Peugeot. First prize in the *concours d'elegance* at Hyères.

and turn naturally and with enthusiasm to the simple truths. When an electric light bulb is at last *weighed*, one fine day, in the design office of a manufacturer of chandeliers, its 50 grams will weigh heavily in the scales that determine the fate of industries doomed to disappearance; the technological firm will replace the artistic: so it is written.

Thus, as new materials and forms were inevitably introduced into the decorative art industries, at the dictate of the all-powerful gods of price and performance, some alert and enquiring minds noted the unvarying laws that were shaping the new products. These laws endowed everything with a common character, and the confidence that they gave to the mind constituted the basis of a new sense of harmony.

If we pause to consider the situation, we are bound to admit that there is no need to wait any longer for objects of utility.

Without a revolution, barricades, or gun-fire, but as a result of simple evolution accelerated by the rapid tempo of our time, we can see decorative art in its decline, and observe that the almost hysterical rush in recent years towards quasi-orgiastic decoration is no more than the final spasm of an already forseeable death.

Ormo steel furniture.

In face of this unbroken and continuing evidence, good sense has gradually rejected the tendency to luxuriousness as inappropriate to our needs. Its last popular resort has been a devotion to *beautiful materials*, which leads to real byzantinism. The final retreat for ostentation is in polished marbles with restless patterns of veining, in panelling of rare woods as exotic to us as humming-birds, in glass pastes, in lacquers copied from *the excesses* of the Mandarins and thence made the starting point for further elaboration. At the same time, the Prefecture of Police has set about pursuing the pedlars of cocaine. This is all of a piece: feverish pulses and nerves shattered in the aftermath of war like to cool themselves by contact with these inhuman materials that keep us at a distance; in other circumstances they could well

16311. FAUTEUIL cintré rustique, gros damas, pieds châtaignier . . **68.** »

16339. TABLE rectangulaire pliante (Touring), peinture jonc ou vert d'eau

| 80/55 | 90 60 | 1ᵐ/60 |
| **46.** » | **52.** .» | **55.** » |

16303.
*CHAISE longue rustique, 2 pièces. monture châtaignier. . . . . **84.** »

16324.
CHAISE TRANSATLANTIQUE, grande taille. toile ordinaire. . **16.** »

Currently available products.

Commercial glassware.

offer us a delicate slice of the miracle of nature; but the matrix of amethyst split and polished, or a lump of rock crystal set on my desk is just as expressive, and a great deal more comfortable as an exemplar of the glittering geometries that enthrall us and that we discover with delight in natural

'Innovation' trunk.

phenomena. When we have occasion to enter one of these troubled sanctuaries where so many artful reflections flit about amongst the black or white marbles, the gilt, the red or blue lacquers, we are seized by malaise, by anguish: we long to leave this den, to escape to the open air, and there, reassured and confident, to seat ourselves in a cell such as that in the convent of Fiesole, or better still, to get down to work in the superb office of a modern factory, which is clear and rectilinear and painted with white ripolin and in which healthy activity and industrious optimism reign.

The religion of beautiful materials is now no more than the final spasm of an agony.

*_**

During these last years we have witnessed the successive stages of a development: with metallic construction, the *separation of decoration from struc-*

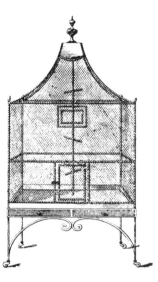

N° 123
Volière rectangulaire
de 60×50, 80×50, 100×50, 110×55

ture. Then the fashion for *expressing the construction*, the sign of a new
construction. Then the ecstasy before *nature*, showing a desire to rediscover
(by however circuitous a path!) the laws of *the organic*. Then the craze for
the *simple*, the first contact with the truths of the machine leading us back to
good sense, and the instinctive manifestation of an aesthetic for our era.

To tie up the final strand: a triggering of our consciousness, a classification, and a normal perception of the objects in our life will emerge, which
distinguishes the highly practical things of work from the intensely free,
living, ideal things of the mind.

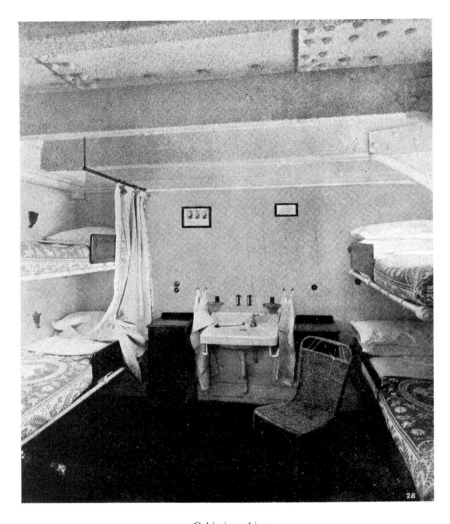

Cabin in a ship.

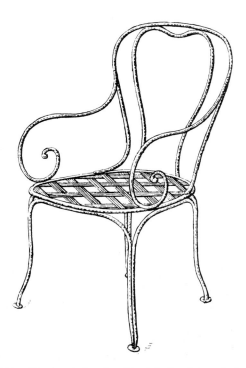

Armchair with a banded seat and back in the shape of a lyre.

EXPO.
ARTS. DECO.

8

The machine, a modern phenomenon, is bringing about a reformation of the spirit across the world.

Nevertheless, the human factor remains intact, since the machine was invented by man to serve human needs.

The machine is conceived within the spiritual framework which man has constructed for himself and not in the realm of fantasy – a framework which forms his tangible universe; this framework, wrested element by element from the world around us, is sufficiently cogent to permit the creation of organs performing functions similar to those of the natural world.

The machine is all geometry. Geometry is our greatest creation and we are enthralled by it.

The machine brings before us shining disks, spheres, and cylinders of polished steel, shaped with a theoretical precision and exactitude which can never be seen in nature itself. *Our senses are moved, at the same time as our heart recalls from its stock of memories the disks and spheres of the gods of Egypt and the Congo. Geometry and gods sit side by side!*

Man pauses before the machine, and the beast and the divine in him there eat their fill.

The lesson of the machine lies in the pure relationship of cause and effect. Purity, economy, the reach for wisdom. A new desire: an aesthetic of purity, of precision, of expressive relationships setting in motion the mathematical mechanisms of our spirit: a spectacle and a cosmogony.

THE LESSON OF THE MACHINE

Paul explained to him his admiration for the machine. His enthusiasm was
keen and his ideas sound, if a little confused. He had been born at the very
moment when the machine itself – the very machine that was to overturn our

existence – was also born. At that time not so far back, one used to say 'as ugly as a machine'. His ideas about art had been developed in a circle of young enthusiasts (his friends), whom Rodin roused to ecstasy. It was the fashion of the time – or let us say more generously, it was a plausible escape from the dead end to which the arts were heading; it was the escape of ship-wrecked mariners who, as they founder, see a phantom ship go by. The awakening is harsh: the safety was illusory. When they became men they quickly saw the worthlessness of Rodin – without having to think too deeply; of Rodin – that is to say, of the cycle of ideas that had formed him. It was in fact a dangerously unbalanced spiritual condition in a world that it was itself unbalanced, its head turned backwards, scrutinising sterile horizons which could never be approached because in fact they were receding – country that had already been crossed.

His adolescence over, came the raw struggles of those who are starting on life. Everything has to be learnt at once, everything is hurled at you at once, to wound you . . . Then the miracle: journeys, some years of chaos, and suddenly a new perspective on things, clean, trenchant, dissentient: 'Ah, now I see it,' said Paul to himself, 'things are not as we are told; they lied to me, those teachers; they clearly saw nothing; they are encrusted with an opaque matrix; I look around and see a world that is organised, that has organised itself, is organising itself, proclaiming itself, shaping itself, polishing itself; a world that has a direction, a direction that determines its laws – laws followed by all who must participate in its affairs.'

Paul, the Bohemian poet, discovers the machine! Man has drawn himself up like a giant, he has forged himself a tool. He no longer works with his hands. His spirit gives the orders. He has delegated to the machine the work of his clumsy and unskilful hands. Freed, his spirit works freely. On squared paper he draws out the daring curves of his dreams. The machine gives reality to his dreams. Man has learnt how to make things *work for him*, calmly, impeccably, unhesitatingly. Holding to the law of immemorial geometry, the geometry of the Egyptians as of the Greeks, he has bred a race of ingenious and fabulously efficient slaves, the machines! He orders the production of artefacts that are polished and absolutely pure – in his own eyes at least; the products pour forth, shining, clean, sharp, as round as ideal spheres, as slender as a lash, as quick as a thunderbolt. The achievement is so miraculous that when these products spring to life, begin to turn, set to work, their motion exceeds our understanding and our powers of perception; our eyes blink, our ears buzz. New organs awake in us, a new diapason, a new vision. 'Man's activity,' concluded Paul, 'is like that of a God – in the realm of perfection.'

His enthusiasm overflowed and he knew the beauty of the machine.

The sensation of pleasure that he received was that of recognizing an organised entity. Organised like living beings, like a powerful or delicate species of animal of astounding ability, that is *never* wrong since its workings are absolute. He pictured the churches abandoned and the lively spirits descended to the place of genesis where beings are remade.

There he re-encountered, in diabolically perfect and immutably exact form, those functions that he had observed in nature and which had brought him joy or terror: the undulations of the snake, the hops of the grasshopper, the majesty of a gliding bird, the fish suspended in the current manoeuvring with the purest harmony, the crab grasping with its pincers, the jaw clenching, the hand gripping, and the foot of a dinosaur that crushes one in a nightmare. His emotions were not paltry, but in constant correlation with poetic sensations experienced when events made him think, and inscribed in his memory the ineradicable trace of the disturbance; the emotions that are our own perceptions of life and that make up our sentient being.

Those were the fundamental machines, the machines with simple functions, the direct expression of kinetics which he understood completely with the simplicity of his intelligence.

Elsewhere he kept quiet before the dismaying complexity of organs and the delicate precision of the titanic power of their movements. He was thunderstruck by a turbine of which he could see no more than the envelope, though he could hear its fearsome roar, because he knew that as a result of this noise, something would now run along those wires, those cables, and bring light and energy to the furthest corners of the country, and death to those who touched them. This light-house beacon by Sauter-Harlé, standing as pure as a negro god, sent out a beam of intense light over fabulous distances on stormy nights at sea. This microscope, gold plate for the monarch of tomorrow, revealed the most unbelieveable things, things that left you troubled. He felt he had woken in a dream, before a miracle, the good God. He mingled all these impressions: at the most recent fair in Paris, presided over by the Eiffel Tower – which he had been told was calculated on the curves of greatest resistance visible in the mysterious but mathematically precise outlines of a longitudinally sectioned femur – he had inspected the mechanical and electrical halls without understanding much; everything overwhelmed him, even the astonishing taste shown in the colours used by engineers to finish off their products.

He was in awe of the precision – precision of coefficient n which had been attained by that time. But he knew well that our children would laugh at this awe in twenty years' time! Their coefficient n would be n^1, a different thing altogether!

He had felt the vertigo of speed, provoked by organs that turned so rapidly one saw no more than a shifting moiré, a rapidity that inspired fear. And he experienced the vertigo of slowness, of rhythms so retarded, yet so

Entire page reserved for
illustration of a lighthouse beacon by
ANCIENS ETABLISSEMENTS SAUTER-HARLÉ
16 Avenue de Suffren
PARIS

TYPICAL STORY OF AN ILLUSTRATION

May 1924. Paris Fair. Electricity Stand. Request for a photo of the big search-light exhibited by Sauter-Harlé. Early July. First phone-call to ask for the document (conversations with several executives, explanation of our objects, means, etc.). Some days later. Second phone-call (same conversations). Some days later. Visit of one of the directors of L'Esprit Nouveau *to the Eta-blissements Sauter-Harlé. Wait for an hour and a half in the waiting-rooms. First engineer, an executive: explanation of the purpose of the visit. Second engineer: second explanation. A very reserved reception: 'Write to the man-agement, to Mr.W. . . , explaining your project, your objects, your means and making it clear that there will be absolutely no charge.'*
Same day: letter sent in full explanation, recalling . . . the stations of the cross!
30th July. Third phone-call. Answer – we don't know.
31st July. Fourth phone-call. Answer – we don't know.
1st August. Fifth phone-call to the manager, Mr.W. . . . General expla-nation. Mr.W. . . . asks for a letter enclosing a copy of the publication, since Mr.R. . . , another manager, has said that he would not give the photo to L'Esprit Nouveau.
Same day, half-an-hour later. Taxi-ride. One of the directors of L'Esprit Nouveau *visits Mr.W. . . . No wait in the waiting-room. Close cross-questioning by Mr.W. . . . followed by an eloquent explanation of objects, means, etc. Mr.W. . . . concludes severely: 'Our lighthouse is not decorative etc . . .' Cutting matters short, he concludes: 'I will telephone on Monday with the outcome of your* request.' *Mr.W. . . . leaves, with no greeting.*
For the last fortnight the Etablissements Sauter-Harlé have been aware that we are going to press with our Number 25, and that today is the last day! Engineers, decked with the pride of numbers, often show this attitude. Total lack of understanding of anything outside their narrow field. Such is the story of one photo, one example among many others equally desperate. There is no communication.

precise, and so far beyond the capability of our own limbs that he felt fear there also.

At 4,000 revolutions per minute the sound was so true that he was ready for a progressive change in his sense of hearing. Paganini was a poor 'failure', he said to himself; the execution of the *Devil's Trill* by human fingers would from now on fall dead on our ears. A player struggling to do it looked distracted; Paul imagined someone watching him with curiosity, then flipping a switch with one motion of his finger to set the turbine spinning; whose the glory now? Proof that virtuosity is far from art, far from eternal values; acrobats belong in the circus where their special abilities are appreciated.

He felt great pride in such a revelation of power. He also discerned in it an objective beauty, a harmony, and even a subjective beauty; *it was something that roused his enthusiasm.*

But Paul felt that his preconceptions, acquired by transfusion from his masters, were opposed to this new development. He was determined to reject them all, but did not yet consider himself ready to judge, assess, or work by himself.

. . . .

He, the companion, had nothing to say against Paul's enthusiams; he shared them himself. But he was too much of an artist not to have searched long for an explanation of the emotion that he also had felt and not, in particular, to have long since sought to triumph over the profound demoralisation that overcame him when, for example, in 1921, he went directly from the *Salon d'Automne* to the *Salon de L'Aéronautique* – both in the Grand Palais: he had felt crushed by the splendour of the machine and had returned to his studio filled with feelings of doubt and negation. He had fought against this by his realisation of the fruitful relationship that could unite the work of art, which was his goal, with the machine, which was the object of his admiration. He tried to pass on to Paul the lesson he had learnt from the machine: the machine is an event of such capital importance in the history of mankind that it is legitimate to credit it with the role of conditioning the human spirit, a role as decisive and more far-reaching than the replacement of one race by another through military conquests over the ages. The machine does not propose one race in lieu of another, but a new world for an old world in the unanimity of all races.

Salon d'Automne.

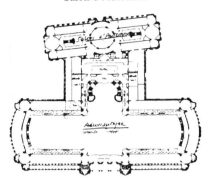

Salon de l'Aéronautique.

The machine, a modern phenomenon, is bringing about a reformation of the spirit across the world. Tangible proof that the evolution which has begun is far from complete is the continuing lack of a universal language, which would break down the cardboard barriers erected along frontiers that from now on are overrun – night-time barriers in a brightening field.

The human factor remains intact, since the machine was invented by man to serve human needs; that is the significant and stable element: the machine is conceived within the spiritual framework which we have constructed for ourselves and not in the realms of fantasy – a framework which forms our tangible universe; this framework, wrested element by element from the world that surrounds us and of which we are a part, is sufficiently cogent to permit the creation of organs performing functions similar to those of the natural world. Reassuring verification.

The miracle of the machine thus lies in having created harmonious organs, that is to say, organs of a harmony that approaches perfection to the extent that they have been purified by experience and invention.

All human endeavours are put to the proof sooner or later, that is to say, once they have registered on the human spirit, on the human heart, on the human conscience; the test may be delayed in matters that affect our emotions; the years pass, men die falsely celebrated or unjustly disparaged; rehabilitation comes late, and so does deserved demotion. In the present confusion of the arts it would be good to shorten this process, protracted and delayed by the innumerable outgrowths sown by the centuries. With the machine the test is immediate; *this one runs, that one does not*! The relationship between cause and effect is direct.

Brown-Boveri.

Broadly, one can say that every machine that runs is a present truth. It is a viable entity, a *clear organism*. I believe that it is towards this clarity, this healthy vitality that our sympathies are directed; paternal feelings: a being has been created that is alive.

But other factors add to these obscure, deep, true feelings. The machine is calculation; calculation is a creative human system that complements our natural abilities, explaining to our eyes the universe of which we are dimly aware by means of its exact analyses, and the nature that we see around us by means of its tangible demonstrations of order in life. The graphical expression of calculation is geometry; calculation is brought into action on the basis of geometry, the means which *is our own*, which is dear to us, and by which alone we can measure events and objects. The machine is all geometry. Geometry is our greatest creation and we are enthralled by it.

The direct mechanism of sight and touch, of the senses, is thus in play. The machine is certainly a marvellous field for experiment in the physiology of the senses, altogether richer and more *ordered* than statuary.

Ordered. Easy comprehension by the eyes; clear perception of the plastic phenomenon that is before your eyes. *Ordered!* Let us reflect for a moment on the fact that there is nothing in nature that, as seen objectively by our eyes, approaches the pure perfection of the humblest machine (the moon is not round; the tree trunk is not straight; only very occasionally are the waters as smooth as a mirror; the rainbow is a fragment; living beings, with very few exceptions, do not conform to the simple geometrical shapes, etc.). If we say with certainty: nature is geometrical, it is not that we have seen it; it is that we have recognized it, that we have interpreted it in accordance with our own framework. And it follows that this is a subjective conclusion.

If we pick up a polished pebble from the sea-shore, choosing the roundest among the millions of others; if we hold in our hand, with the pose of a statue, a piece of fruit that is almost spherical, etc., it is because we aspire to the attainment of geometry. The machine thus appears to us the goddess of beauty. And that is no more than sincere but *misdirected* enthusiasm (because we then think of it in terms of a 'work of art').

But in place of the calcareous pebble or the imperfect orange, the machine brings shining before us disks, spheres, the cylinders of polished steel, polished more highly *than we have ever seen before*: shaped with a theoretical precision and exactitude *which can never be seen in nature itself*. Our hand reaches out to it, and our sense of touch *looks* in its own way as our fingers close round it. Our senses are moved at the same time as our heart recalls from its stock of memories the disks and spheres of the gods of Egypt and the Congo. Gods! Geometry and gods sit side by side (an old human story, truth to tell, the basic and original human story).

Machines beget machines. They are now abundant, and they can be seen gleaming everywhere. Their polish is on the sections. The sections reveal the geometry that controls everything. If we polish the sections, it is to reach for their functional perfection. The spirit of perfection shines out at points of geometrical perfection.

It is essentially for this reason that man pauses before the machine to admire it. The beast and the divine in him there eat their fill.

But the machines are adorned with colour, with grey, with vermilion, with green, with blue. Grey on the complex castings, bright colours on the pure geometry of the sections.

Now think of works of plastic art (the enfeebled plastic art of the end of the pre-machine era): confronted by the machine, your lyricism will transport you beyond the bounds of prudent restraint.

Set the machine in motion. All gates open, all is a confusion of joy. *It should well be remembered that we are the first generation in the millennia of time to see the machine*, and such enthusiasm should be forgiven us.

The lesson of the machine lies in the pure relationship of cause and effect. Purity, economy, the reach for wisdom.

Our awakening to *the intense joys of geometry* is brutal, because overwhelming. Now we can feel them with our senses (whilst Copernicus and Archimedes could do no more than discover them with their heads).

The rule of precision. Cause-effect. *Salon de L'Aéronautique* as opposed to *Salon d'Automne*! Now let us apply our ideas to the plastic art that has come down to us in this searing hour of the machine. Confusion! Neurasthenia! This art, whose last dregs are hung out along our picture rails in a tattered fringe, is not the art of the modern phenomenon that captures our imagination. Revolt. Would there be aesthetic revolution? It would become normal for man to conceive, for his inspiration, a sequence of *disinterested* works unlike any machine, but animated by a mathematical sensibility ordering pure forms in pure relationships. A page would have been turned on that day, for a moment showing our troubled eye no more than a narrow edge, so that it could see nothing. Tomorrow the turn will be complete, and the heavy hand of the new truth will crush the past beneath the turned page.

A great adventure it may be, on which we are now embarked without hesitation and almost without heed. We still have our feet planted *on yesterday*.

So errors are committed: exaggeration, immoderation, disharmony. Art has no business resembling a machine (the error of *Constructivism*). But our eyes are enthralled by pure forms. The means of art (whose objective is constant, eternal, human emotion) are set free, illumined with clarity.

A new desire; an aesthetic of purity, of precision, of expressive relationships setting in motion the mathematical mechanisms of our spirit: a spectacle and a cosmogony.

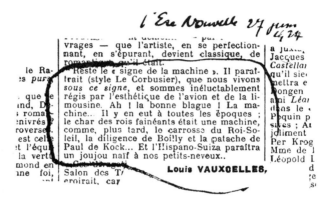

l'Ère Nouvelle 27 juin 24

vrages — que l'artiste, en se perfectionnant, en s'épurant, devient classique, de romantique qu'il était.

Reste le « signe de la machine ». Il paraîtrait (style Le Corbusier), que nous vivons *sous ce signe*, et sommes inéluctablement régis par l'esthétique de l'avion et de la limousine. Ah ! la bonne blague ! La machine... Il y en eut à toutes les époques ; le char des rois fainéants était une machine, comme, plus tard, le carrosse du Roi-Soleil, la diligence de Boilly et la pataché de Paul de Kock... Et l'Hispano-Suiza paraîtra un joujou naïf à nos petits-neveux..

Louis VAUXCELLES,

Salon des T/

9

Decorative art can no longer exist any more than can the 'styles' themselves.

In relation to the style of an age, the 'styles' are no more than an accidental surface modality, superadded to facilitate composition, stuck on to disguise faults, or duplicated for the sake of display.

If decorative art has no reason to exist, tools on the other hand do exist, and there exist also architecture and the work of art.

A tool, something that gives service, a servant, a menial. A single requirement: that it serves well.

Architecture is a construct of the mind which gives material form to the sum consciousness of its age.

The work of art, the living 'double' of a being, whether still present, or departed, or unknown; that moment of profound discourse; those open and eloquent words spoken in the intimacy of the soul; perhaps this Sermon on the Mount.

Decorative art lies far from these paths; to attempt to define its position is to reveal clearly its purpose and different orientation: that of providing decoration, of promoting decorum.

The work of art grows ever more concentrated.

We feel ourselves disposed to respect the work of art.

The hour of architecture sounds, now that art awaits from the spirit of our age its definition in material form, now that decorative art can no longer be considered compatible with the framework of contemporary thought.

Nimba, negro god. Trocadero Museum.

RESPECT FOR WORKS OF ART

Decorative art can no longer exist any more than can the 'styles' themselves.

In relation to the style of an age, the 'styles' are no more than an accidental surface modality, superadded to facilitate composition, stuck on to disguise faults, or duplicated for the sake of display. Display is not very becoming, except for kings; the citizen abhors display and the thinking man thinks better in a space where the air flows freely.

But if decorative art has no reason to exist, tools on the other hand do exist, and there exist also architecture and the work of art.

A tool, something that gives service: a servant, a menial; a piece of domestic equipment. One single requirement: that it serves well.

Architecture is a construct of the mind which gives material form to the sum consciousness of its age.

The work of art, the 'living double' of a being, whether still present, or departed, or unknown; that faithful mirror of an individual passion; that moment of profound discourse; that confession of a like mind, those open and eloquent words spoken in the intimacy of the soul; perhaps this *Sermon on the Mount*.

There is always art. Art is inseparable from being, a truly indissoluble source of exaltation with the power to bestow pure happiness. It is intimately linked to the movements of our heart, and it makes the stages of our difficult path through the thickets of this age and all ages, towards a state of awareness. It guides us through time, from the moment when we are crushed by an immense and dominating nature, to that moment of serenity when we have learnt to understand her and to work in harmony with her law; the passage from the age of subjection to the age of creation – the history of civilisation, as also the history of the individual. The arts are an eloquent mirror which reflects the indices of power of each epoch as well as the coefficients that express the emotions of the soul.

The folk cultures are born; overpowering nature inspires terror and anxiety or, without affectation, reveals the beauty of her thousand little flowers.

From time to time a moment of revelation, of grace, raises the general level: Giotto, Michelangelo . . .

Periods of high consciousness, of self-possession, of stoicism, denote the apogees: a Parthenon is built.

How then can one assign a legitimate place between these two banks that delimiting the course of the soul – on one side the fear of the unexplained, on the other the serenity of knowledge – to *decorative art*, something which touches only the surface – chatter and sweet nothings? One cannot assign a place to decorative art on this sincere, touching, and passionate course, alongside the folk cultures and the work of art. Decorative art lies far from it; to attempt to define its position is to reveal clearly its purpose and quite different orientation: that of providing decoration, of

ATHENA PARTHENOS OF PHIDIAS
(reduced scale).

National Museum, Athens.

Papua.

promoting decorum. It thus comes down to a judgement on quality of thought, to a categorisation of what decorates or promotes decorum.

The shepherd who shapes his staff and carves into it an annulet of flowers and stars, a snake, or a lamb; the Papuan who inscribes on his paddle the figure of an albatross and a surging wave; they are both making an act of devotion towards nature. The practice of their art has amassed the experience of generations and their candid works have thus passed beyond the level of superficial observation to that of true re-creation. Integration. The thought and work of human kind!

Greek vase-painting.

The Greek or Etruscan who has perfected the vigorous lines of an acanthus on the sides of a vase has not only conceived a microcosm of botany, but has given expression to the architecture of creation, the organising breath that animates all living beings from the roots to the fruit that falls. Decoration of this kind bears witness to man's understanding of the nature of life.

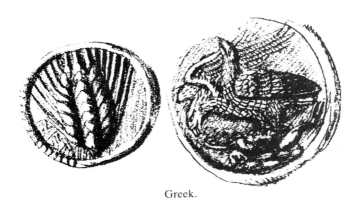

Greek.

Following the same pattern of development towards a type, the Greek medallist has made an effigy from an ear of corn, and a poem full of lofty nobility from a pair of eagles. Folk culture, in which the particular is absorbed in the general, has here been surpassed, and the expression of an individual passion can be felt – the convulsion and emotion from which flows the perception of a relationship.

And so here is lyricism at its most absolute, the quintessence extracted from the natural phenomenon, the force of pure meaning; the complete realisation of a relationship established between certain human emotions: the crescent moon, the star, the sword-blade.

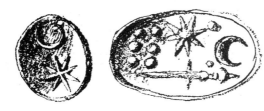

The need for art, which is apparent from the very beginning of human activity, leads the soul along the path from candid observation of the spectacle of nature to the lyrical synthesis of the symbol – a symbol that is nevertheless explicit. One step further leads to the world of hermeticism, outside art; one step less and art has not been attained, for the expression of human intervention is not complete.

Peoples, individuals give their utmost – the maximum of which they are capable: dry observation of the natural phenomena of which they have experience, creativity in proportion to their technical and spiritual resources. Depending on their latitude, depending on their youthful vigour or their exhaustion, and depending on whether their arts spring from the country or the city, their level of expression varies between direct imitation and the most reconstructed forms of figuration.

* *
*

There are three clear stages: *archaism*, in which the inadequacy of means prevents full realisation of the dream; but a plastic imperative, a plastic mechanism inseparable from the foundations of our being gives magnificent support to the idea, which is still no more than a germ but is imbued with concentrated power. *Naturalism*, which is the moment of knowledge, the achievement of self-awareness, of analysis, of overflowing wealth, of passionate rationalism; an intoxicating hour – but less grandiose than the unselfconscious art that preceded it, and less notable, less elevated than the disinterested art that is to follow. *Hieratism*, which is the hour of full knowledge, of mastery over means, the exact hour of choice, of rejection of the superfluous, of concentration, of abnegation, the supreme moment of exaltation, the platform of great art – of the work of art, both immense and simple, stripped down but crammed with inner richness, exact and precise, perfectly balanced.

The *Medieval*, which won its place in the world by its vivacity, goes beyond folk culture through observation and the exercise of free will; everywhere it examines the teeming world that surrounds it, and everything affords a pretext for the fever of generosity that troubles it: on the stalls of Amiens cathedral there is a wooden carving of a herd of cattle, whose uncontrolled mass overflows the limits which a more pedestrian imagination had assigned to it.

The *Romanesque*, the prolongation of a marvellous civilisation, now come up against the limits of the symbolic; it reflects the continuing influence of mathematics, albeit heavily, but everywhere its healthy and vital forces manage to synthesize the forces of nature: the bud that bursts.

Gothic. Amiens.

The *Egyptian* had also stylised the forces of nature: but within the high priestly caste subtle relationships linked the eagle, the snake, and the winged bull, implying esoteric mysteries which for us still entail an inescapable poetic disquiet.

Romanesque. The church of Poissy.

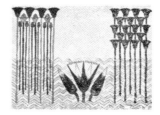

Egyptian.

· ·

So there is a clear line of descent from the naïve works sprung from the bud to those which attain to relationships of great sensitivity.

That is the human contribution, a significant attainment, profound, austere, *serious*.

What place in it could there be for the futility of decoration, of decorum?

If decoration and decorum are part of our everyday life, and have always been so, they yet have no part in the lineal descent of art; they serve a certain caste of persons who practise decorum. This caste has had no aware-

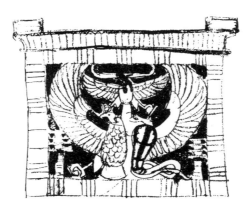

Egyptian.

ness of the harsh and beautiful passage of the soul through the disquiet that dwells within us.

* * *

So we see the compass of human emotion extending from the bud to the sword-blade and the star, from a primary symbol to a subtle relationship: a stage in culture, an advance.

The twentieth century: science, books, popularisation.

Je sais tout, *Science et Vie*, *Sciences* and *Voyages* disect the cosmic phenomenon before our eyes: stunning, revealing, disturbing photographs, or emotive diagrams, graphs, tables.

Here, in widespread use in books, schools, newspapers, and at the cinema, is the language of our emotions that was in use *in the arts* for thousands of years before the twentieth century.

We are at the dawn of the machine age. A new consciousness disposes us to look for a different aesthetic satisfaction from that afforded by the bud carved on the capitals in churches. We have learnt about such things from science books and have a much more extensive and precise scientific knowledge of them. We are brought face to face with the phenomenon of the cosmos through treatises, documentary pictures, and graphs. We derive the same emotion from it as the shepherd, but our investigations go deeper and introduce us to the mathematical basis of the world.

The documentation presented by the cinema, books, *Je sais tout*, *Science et Vie*, has taken over a whole field formerly the prerogative of poetry. We now approach the mystery of nature scientifically, and far from exhausting it, we find it becomes more profound for every advance in our knowledge. This is the developing culture of our age.

As for esoteric symbols, they subsist for the initiates of today in the curves that represent forces and the formulas that resolve the phenomena of nature.

Our enquiries, our questions are met by the thousand answers of science.

But science provides us, furthermore, with tools of the most astounding precision, beyond the dreams of all ages since the creation of the world. We can have everything, and we cater to our needs with every imaginable aid: our comfort is assured.

In reality, we have in no way added to our satisfaction unless our spirit is nourished and our heart enriched.

Freed from the cosmic dread assuaged by books, we attain to the pure realm of the work of art, which consists in nothing more than significant relationships between expressive elements, provokers of feeling. Elegant relationships, brutal relationships, powerful relationships – important events of intellectual quality that are as indispensable for some people as bread.

The loss of folk culture will leave a void around us – a void whose silence will favour inner work. The work of art will find there its atmosphere. By not disturbing this atmosphere, we will show the respect for the work of art that is its due.

* *
*

And how will this atmosphere be created, except by architecture, whose objective is to create relationships?

* *
*

The work of art grows ever more concentrated.

We feel ourselves disposed to respect the work of art.

Khmer sculpture.*
Khmer Sculpture, by H. Marchal & O. Miestchaninoff. Librairie de France.

The hour of architecture sounds, now that art awaits from the spirit of our age its definition in material form, now that decorative art can no longer be considered compatible with the framework of contemporary thought.

1925

EXPO.

ARTS. DÉCO.

10

Great art lives by humble means.
Glitter is going under.
The hour of proportion has arrived.
The spirit of architecture is asserting itself.
What has occurred? A machine age has been born.
Our effusions and our vivid awareness of the beauties and power of nature have found their place within the framework of architecture. For science, by revealing to us the phenomenon of the universe, has placed great power in our hands, and architecture is the necessary condition for human creation.

The *Dixmude*.

THE HOUR OF ARCHITECTURE

Now that the decorative arts are in decline, justice demands recognition for the service records of several generations of active, enthusiastic, disinterested people.

If the accelerated pace of our times is hastening the development of a new, pure consciousness, it is right to inscribe on the roll of honour those whose work has been indispensable in bringing it about.

Decorative art has raised from its cradle the new consciousness born of the machine and has thrust into the background the inert, blind masses, lost in ignorance of the hour, who brought the pre-machine epoch to an inglorious end.

The spirit which is awakening, springing up full of wonder, fighting against suffocation, winning its place and, as the days dawn, affirming itself in the clarity of an ideal precisely formulated, because precisely conceived – this spirit was first enlisted under the banner of decorative art. It is worth pointing that out and according it recognition; justice demands that the butterfly, as it steps out of its chrysalis, should say not only goodbye, but *thank you*.

As children, we were exhorted by Ruskin. A paradoxical prophet, laboured, complex, contradictory. It was an intolerable period that could not last; a time of crushing bourgeois values, sunk in materialism, bedecked with idiotic mechanical decoration, made by machines which, to the acclamation of Homais, poured out papier-mâché and cast-iron foliage in an unstoppable flow. Ruskin spoke of spirituality. In his *Seven Lamps of Architecture** shone the Lamp of Sacrifice, the Lamp of Truth, the Lamp of Humility.

He gave a demonstration of honesty to a population gorged with the first fruits of the nascent machine age: go to San Giovanni e Paolo in Venice and take a very long ladder with you; lean it against the grandest tomb – that of Vendramin; climb to the top of the ladder and look at the head of Vendramin, seen in profile as it lies on the catafalque. Lean over and look at the other side of the head, behind the profile. *This other side is not carved.* Disaster! Cheating! Falsehood! Treason! Everything is false in this sumptuous, enormous tomb. This tomb is the work of the devil. Hasten to the archives of Venice and you will find that the sculptor who was so royally paid to raise this magnificent tomb was a forger and was expelled from Venice for forging documents!

That was how Ruskin shook our young minds profoundly with his exhortation.

Grasset was the geometrician and algebraist of flowers. With him we had to extend our admiration for all flowers as far as the secret of their structure, to love them so much that there was no alternative but to scatter them over all the works that we would like to have undertaken. Our childhood was illuminated by the miracles of nature. Our hours of study were spent hunched over a thousand flowers and insects. Trees, clouds and birds were the field of our research; we tried to understand their life-curve, and con-

*First published in London in 1849. J.I.D.

cluded that only nature was beautiful and that we could be no more than humble imitators of her forms and her wonderful materials.

Ruskin examined the floral decoration on the capitals of the Ducal Palace, and in the porticoes and stalls of its cathedral he traced the 'Bible of Amiens'; while Grasset, with a flower in his hand and the dissecting scalpel of the botanist at the ready, was establishing the *Grammar of Ornament*.

We had been told: Go and explore in the calm of the library the great compendium by Owen Jones, the *History of Ornament**. This, without question, was a serious business. The pure ornaments which man had created entirely out of his head followed one another in sequence. Yes, but what we found there was overwhelmingly man as part of nature, and if nature was omnipresent, man was an integral part of it, with his faculties of crystallisation and his geometrical formation. From nature we moved on to man. From imitation to creation. This book was beautiful and true, for in it everything was summed up that had been made, that in a profound sense had been *achieved*: the decoration of the Savage, the decoration of the Renaissance Man, of the Gothic, the Romanesque, the Roman, the Chinese, the Indian, the Greek, the Assyrian, the Egyptian, etc. With this book we felt that the problem was posed: Man *creates what moves him*.

The mentality of our parents was the antithesis of art. The monument to Meissonnier was just being finished. That was all. Ruskin, William Morris and Walter Crane were founding a press to produce *beautiful books* (and heaven knows how disagreeable this frank return to the missals of the Middle Ages is to us). Then at the Paris Exhibition of 1900, a dazzling handful of those works was displayed in which nature, giving geometry time off for a rest cure, twists the life out of those building and craft materials which normally suffer from it. But it represented a superb effort, considerable courage, enormous daring, a true revolution. In 1900 fire took hold of our souls. People began then to talk about Decorative Art. And skirmishes broke out: great art, minor arts. Two camps.

Houses were dreamed up with the rhythm of the living stem of wild clematis (Gallé). The past was searched for evidence, and in anything floral, in all direct observation of plants and animals, Gothic was held in esteem. Water, earth and sky, the Botanic Gardens and the Natural History Museum – they were all there to be explored with ineffable love for the creatures of the Good Lord. Ruskin had softened our hearts.

Elsewhere other problems were being discussed without emotion, the problems of structure: there, architecture put down roots.

Then came the crazes for the exotic: China, Japan, India, Persia. To affirm the values of the West now required some energy.

Gallé had a fine time, divided between the direct study of nature and the whims of his kilns. He left objects which are beautiful creations, plastic and

---

*This is not quite clear. *The Grammar of Ornament* by Owen Jones (London, 1856) must be meant. Eugéne Grasset published *La Plante et ses applications* in 1900, and *Méthode de composition* in 1905. J.I.D.

sensitive . . . so very sensitive, so much the antithesis of the present-day output of the decorative arts, which have deserted nature and returned to the archaeology of Louis-Philippe or the Second Empire. Gallé was a laudable man, and his work is laudable.

Objects lovingly shaped, materials snatched from the fire – when all is said and done, there was emotion, an outpouring, what one can all 'sincerity'. Such purity of heart has an impact on opinion, as the preaching of Ruskin had already had its impact. Opinion became preoccupied with decorative art. Precious and useless works came to take their place in the glass cases alongside Japanese curios.

Curios there certainly were. There was a growing public that liked to run its hands over good examples exuding the aura of flowers and untrammelled nature. Meanwhile Otto Wagner in Vienna and de Baudot and Auguste Perret in Paris aspired to equip architecture with new means and were ready to throw all traditional aesthetic practices into the melting-pot. These signs gave hope to the proponents of the movement. There was a hullabaloo. Curiosity was awakened. An enormous literature was born. Magazines carried a taste for the arts into the home.

So young ladies became crazy about decorative art – poker-work, metal-work, embroidery. Girls' boarding schools made room for periods of Applied Art and the History of Art in their timetables.

At this point it looked as if decorative art would founder among the young ladies, had not the exponents of the *decorative ensemble* wished to show, in making their name and establishing their profession, that male abilities were indispensable in this field: considerations of *ensemble*, organisation, sense of unity, balance, proportion, harmony.

There were the germs of architecture in this. Immense success followed. The *ensembliers* were right. Some of the questions of architecture were being dealt with in their work; elsewhere, around 1912, Loos wrote that sensational article, *Ornament and Crime*, and Auguste Perret was building the Garage Ponthieu (1906).

One heard it said: 'An ornament generally conceals a defect in construction.'

Proof that there was an effort to build well.

Now, when a new system of construction comes out of its wrappings there are great moments of anguish. Even if one can make it *stand up*, one is often confronted with formidable difficulties when it comes to getting the new system of construction to *form a complete whole*. To get it to form a complete whole means to dispose everything perfectly at the same time, both in the structural system and the plastic system. Reason and emotion inflexibly demand the 'complete product'. Rome was not made in a day. Think of the twenty year evolution of the motor car. Reinforced concrete left some uncertainties, some lacunae. It went on being decorated. The plastic system, which should flow naturally from a system of construction, was still unclear. This search for a plastic *system* for reinforced concrete brings us to the present time. That is where we stand.

Now all these efforts, and the crusade mounted by the Ruskins, Grassets and Gallés, had by this time made a profound impression, and as the hour of architecture was about to strike – the conclusion of a century of work with machines – a great shift in public opinion had been achieved: attention was focused on architecture.

The designers of decorative ensembles sense that the time is past for decoration. They no longer make furniture shaped like the stem of the wild clematis. Architects no longer pore over the 'Bible of Amiens'. That is out. Both of them would sooner go for Louis-Philippe and 'modern Louis XVI', now that they have come out against decoration.

However, as a by-product of the new-born architecture, a taste for polychromy is joyfully running riot. Colour for its own sake has really caught the imagination. Symphony of colours, triumph of the decorative ensemble. Colours and materials. Colour used for display. Now that one is involved in it, one might as well do it well. Some fine mixtures have been cooked up. Colours, materials.

What shimmering silks, what fancy, glittering marbles, what opulent bronzes and golds! What fashionable blacks, what striking vermilions, what silver lamés from Byzantium and the Orient! Enough.

Such stuff founders in a narcotic haze. Let's have done with it.

We will soon have had more than enough.

It is time to crusade for whitewash and Diogenes.

***

It is interesting all the same to take stock of fifty years of development and see where we have come from and where we are going!

Whitewash. Diogenes. The hour of architecture. Truth, the sense of truth. And plasticity. For, under this aegis, the means are frail and the will must be strong. Great art lives by humble means.

Glitter is going under.

The hour of proportion has arrived.

There are now signs that it is emerging almost everywhere – in America, Russia, Germany, Czechoslovakia, Holland, France – there are houses free from decoration where the problems of proportions and structure are posed.

Decoration is dead and the spirit of architecture is asserting itself.

What has really happened? The machine-age has been born, and, except for the rising generation of twenty-year olds, all our feet are mired in

Fabre, the entomologist.

the agony of the previous age. We expended our manhood on seeing clearly, on grasping the meaning of what was coming, on spring-cleaning . . . and how! Around 1880 the factories were black with soot, the machines ugly and filthy, and they turned out cast-iron leaf-ornament and *papier-mâché* borders in profusion and almost for nothing. Industrialists with large whiskers extending railways everywhere were engaged in acts of mental cruelty, for everything had to be pushed aside: the peasants would fire on the trains as they advanced into the fields. The *Forge-master*, etc., Zola! etc. No art, oh no, not at all, not the least thought for that sort of thing. The poets were disgusted and indignant. Huysmans' *The Cathedral*. And also his *Against Nature*. The machine was hideous; the age is prostrate before it, the world was collapsing, etc. Protests. The past was regarded with longing.

The sweet voice of Ruskin – 'Look, here are the flowers, the insects, and the beasts of the Good Lord.' Soul of Giotto. Delight in primitives. *Pre-Raphaelitism*. Here in rational France the appeal to nature; analysis. The entomologist Fabre excited us.* We realised that natural phenomena have an organisation, and *we opened our eyes*. 1900. An outpouring. Truly, a fine moment!

Then Germany, working twenty-four hours a day, seized the moment. Her painters built houses – Darmstadt and after. But houses have no life without structure. All that great noise was for nothing. Nothing came out of it all. Still, it was a stimulus. The Munich people came to Paris in 1912. The Salon d'Automne. The *ensembliers*. 1914: the event that upset everything. Then it was just a question of bullets. In our minds also. Everything was said and done. The old world was shattered, trampled on, rejected, buried. Cubism, so profoundly serious in the hands of its authors, is evidence that everything was called into question. Around 1910 it already showed the pressures for revolt and the ascetic virility appropriate to conspirators bent on overturning the established order. This was achieved. While the affair took its course, technology could dare everything. The technology of building was purified. The framework became clearer.

A new conception has been born. Decoration is no longer possible. Our effusions, our vivid awareness of the beauties and power of nature have found their place within the framework of architecture.

Architecture is there, concerned with our home, our comfort, and our heart. Comfort and proportion. Reason and aesthetics. Machine and plastic form. Calm and beauty.

---

*Jean-Henri Fabre, who published his *Souvenirs entomologiques* in 1870–89, chiefly noted for his observations of social relationships among insects. J.I.D.

11

The Eiffel Tower has been accepted as architecture.

In 1889 it was seen as the aggressive expression of mathematical calculation.

In 1900 the aesthetes wanted to demolish it.

In 1925 it dominated the Exhibition of Modern Decorative Arts. Above the plaster palaces writhing with decoration, it stood out pure as crystal.

Photo Stavba.

MILESTONES

1914: the event that upset everything.
 Then it was just a question of bullets. In our minds also. Everything was said and done. The old world was shattered, trampled on, rejected, buried.

It was over and done with. While the event took its course, technology could dare everything.

Technology.

The decorative arts were anti-technology. Their efforts were directed to opposite ends from the common effort of the age. They aimed to restore manufacture by hand. The physical products of decorative art have no place within the context of the age.

But the spiritual convulsion has led – painfully, slowly, with all its regrets and backward glances – to clarification. The spirit, always quick to respond, has yet to emerge from an orgy of frenetic divination (futurism, expressionism, constructivism). It is still feverish, but this time there is promise of a cure and of an assured advance in the direction of the age.

The spirit is also already directing its gaze beyond the fever to the pure zones of harmony . . .

Tomorrow will see . . . thanks to purifying technology.

Why doubt that tomorrow can have perfect harmony – new as it will be, a unified creation, a whole constituted from the elements of the present but unencumbered with the trappings of the previous age.

Standing behind us today are the *milestones*. Each has added its word to the violence of the spiralling phrase, which has its basis in the past, but today sets us in opposition to that past.

The images which follow are the milestones:

1898   Chéret and the music hall.

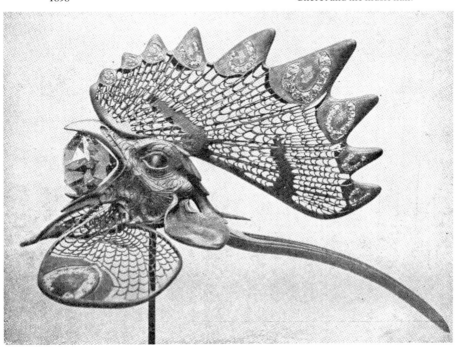

1900   Lalique.

1899   Guimard.

1902   Plumet et Selmersheim.

1902   R. d'Aronco.

1902   Peter Behrens.

1903   E. Grasset.

1904   P. Follot.

1904   Hoffmann.

1904   Salmersheim.

1908   Lenoble.

1906   Delaherche.

1908   E. Robert.

1909   Sézille.

1910   Veil.

1910   Jaulmes.

1911   P. Follet.

1910   Carriès.

1912   Lalique.

1911   Bakst.

1913   A. et G. Perret.

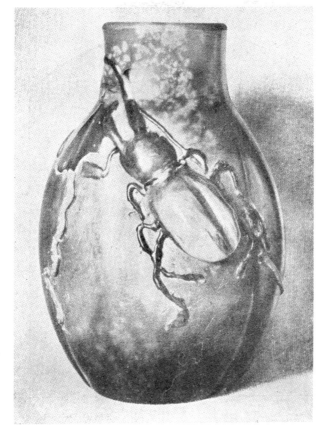

1911   Gallé.

1913   Mallet-Stevens.

1913   Süe et Palyart.

1913   Jallot.

1919   Martine.

1919   Süe et Mare.

1920   Voisin house (aeroplanes) (Noël et Patout).

1920   Picasso. Décor for the ballet *The Three-Cornered Hat*.

1921 P. Follot.

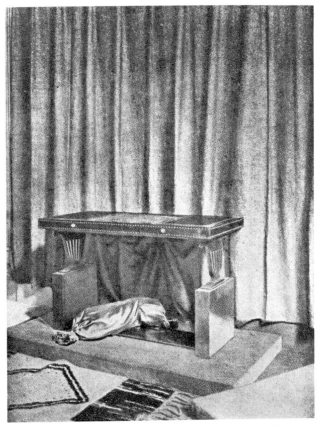

1920 Ruhlman.

1921   The liner *Paris*.

1921   Brandt (The liner *Paris*).

L'Illustré

Tamara Karsawina.

Photo Kerstone View London

Mn. Mistinguette.

1922   Ch. Plumet.

1921   M. Dufrène.

1923   Francis Jourdain.

1923   P. Charean.

NOTE: This series of pictures, which covers a period of 25 years, comes from the collection of *Art et Décoration*, the only decorative arts magazine which has spanned the last quarter-century without break.

1925

EXPO.

ARTS. DÉCO.

12

Even before the formulation of a theory, the emotion leading to action can be felt: theory later gives support to sentiment in a variety of seemingly incontrovertible ways.

An active being carries with him the sense of truth, which is his power of judgement. It is an imperative which is at the same time his force and his lucidity. The sense of truth is the strength of a man.

In respect of our work, of human labour, of the human world, nothing exists or has the right to exist, that has no explanation. We set to work: our intention must be clear because we are not madmen. We work for a purpose . . . however crass it may be.

I notice that a whole mass of objects which once bore the sense of truth have lost their content and are now no more than carcasses: I throw them out.

I will throw out everything from the past except that which is still of service to me. Some things are always of service: art.

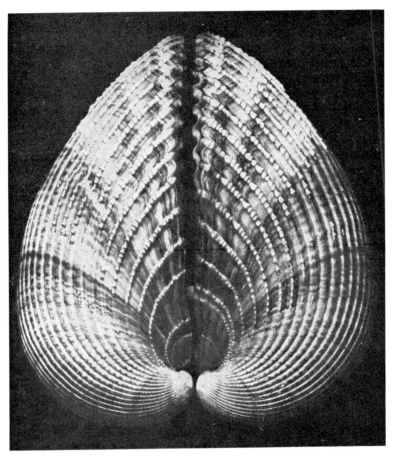

Photo 'Wendingen'.

THE SENSE OF TRUTH

Whitewash, Diogenes . . . The hour of architecture. Truth, sense of truth . . .

Diogenes, throwing away his bowl, had said 'This child shows me that I still have something I can do without.'

To identify the superfluous and throw it away.

The superfluous is something that serves no purpose.

Everything which moves us serves a purpose. Everything that obstructs is surplus to needs. What is not superfluous? The essential.

One moment, here come the sophists: 'Everything serves a purpose, everything moves us.'

Answer: 'There are only twenty-four hours in a day.'

That is indisputable, unchangeable, the constant. That is the arbiter of everything. You cannot be moved by everything: you don't have time for it. You have to choose.

So you have to define what is essential, what is superfluous, the twenty-four hour day by itself fixes the meaning of the word *superfluous* and the word *essential*.

But, when the sophists persisted, Diogenes began doing his hundred paces in front of Zeno, who denied the reality of movement and insisted on proving it . . .

Santa Sophia in Constantinople.

From our inner depths, before even the formulation of a theory, the emotion leading to action can be felt: reason then gives support to feeling in a variety of seemingly incontrovertible ways. Feeling perceives and reason confirms. Feeling makes one act. So let no one accuse me of wanting to kill feeling.

So I think that not everything serves a purpose, that not everything moves us.

Child's drawing.

* * *

After many years of participation in exciting and hopeless ventures, after filling our time like countless modest people with aimless movements, we chance on an experience that gives us a rational faith, a faith like St Thomas' – the St Thomas who wanted to touch with his finger. It is a faith acquired through experience: *it is a sense of truth*. Things exist because they have a reason, because they work. Something exists: only on condition that it can be read, can be analysed, can be understood.

Feeling dominates. Feeling is never extinguished by reason. Reason gives feeling the purified means it needs to express itself in its essentials. Here are three boats answering the same requirements. Three races have created their own types. The lyrical feeling of each race is expressed with all its force.

Photos Leyckam. . . . living beings that we have created.

Simplistic rationalism? Yes perhaps, if it was indiscriminately applied. But for the present we are most certainly not in the agora of the philosophers: we are only dealing with decorative art.

Besides, Cocteau has shown us delightfully how to let off steam: like it or not, there is always space for our curios and room for mystery.

'– And railway accidents, Lord? What is your explanation for railway accidents?'

GOD (put out) – 'Things like that can't be explained, they can only be felt'.[1]

If I feel myself spurred on by this sense of truth, which is a kind of imperative, it is not that the sensitive side of my nature is in any way repressed. On the contrary, it is because it has become active. No one will class me definitively among the heartless and soulless because I doubt decorative art, because my good sense does not allow me to tolerate easily those futile objects which, whether the labour they demanded was sincere or not, howl or murmur around me, fill my air-space, cramp my movements,

1. Cocteau.

Photos *L'Illustré*.

Photos *L'Illustré*.

Photo Leyckam.

steal precious minutes from me, occupy an enormous – or even a limited – space in the twenty-four hours of an already short day. I claim the right to be harsh with these objects that serve no purpose, that are superfluous, that are not essential.

Section of a cable.

* * *

In nature, in the concatenation of events, in everything – I know it well – we are confronted by the inescapable:
    'Everything serves a purpose.'
    'Everything moves us.'
    'Everything is inexplicable.' Of course!

The inexplicability of cause. But everywhere, in nature as in events, an explanation of the concatenation exists. Going back to the limit of our awareness, we can find the reasons. The further back we go, the more satis-

faction we obtain. We learn that everything is arranged according to principles consistent with the whole: that every organism is a kind of link in the chain of variants around the axis between two poles, variants which, responding to a single factor, establish a series: a coherent system varies in

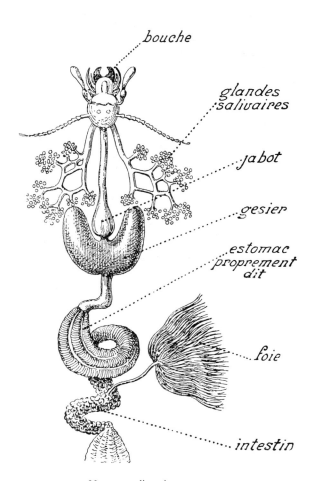

bouche

*glandes
salivaires*

jabot

gesier

*estomac
proprement
dit*

foie

intestin

Nature: a digestive system.

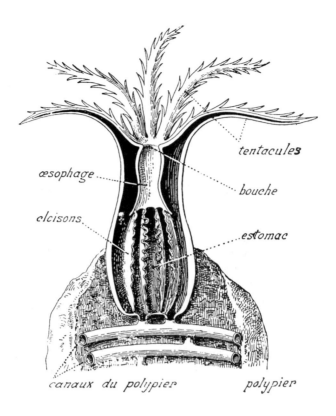

tentacule**s**

œsophage

bouche

clcisons

estomac

canaux du polypier   polypier

accordance with the countless possible sets of combination. The world is then shaken down to a few species. The laws of physics subject these systems to a fatal process of selection.

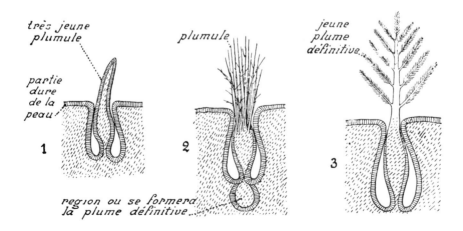

très jeune plumule

partie dure de la peau

region ou se formera la plume définitive

1

plumule

2

jeune plume définitive

3

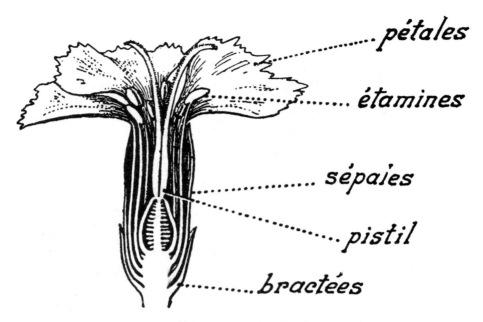

pétales

étamines

sépales

pistil

bractées

Nature: organs which function.

Destinies, causes, reasons? A mystery: not our business.

Nature and external events are separate from our creativity; they are outside; they happen to cross our path. But in respect of our work, of human labour, of human organisation, of the human world – nothing exists or has the right to exist that has no explanation. We set to work: our intention must be clear, because we are not madmen. We work for a purpose . . . however crass it may be.

The gondola of an airship.

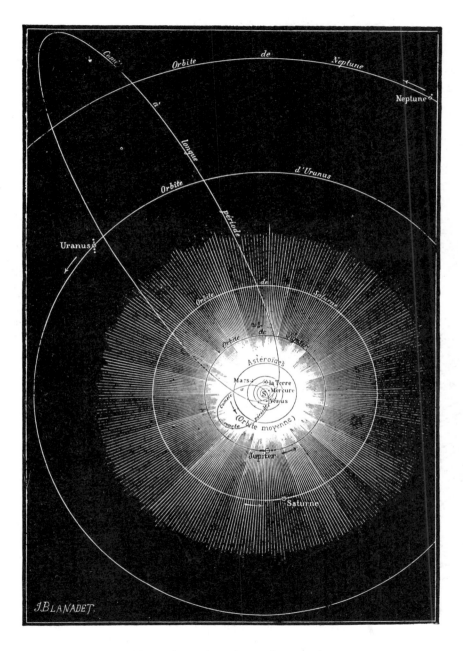

What we know about the creation around us.

The inexplicable arises in the relationship between our activity and the universe. It is here that the artist comes in, at the same time posing and resolving the emotional question. But if I feel emotion, I have yet to explain why I am moved by works that are explicable.

Under analysis, the explicable works survive – those that have a truth in themselves, a truth proceeding from the human mind.

To judge it, I possess this sense of truth which is a yardstick. Then I can explain. Even if the objects which I try to explain are beyond my comprehension, I explain to myself where my deficiency lies, and insofar as the work *serves a purpose*, I reckon that it is explicable and legitimate. Then my action is determined by a judgement. I accept nothing if I cannot discover a reason for it. As a worker I take note of things which work: I surround myself with them. One day I notice that a whole mass of objects which once bore the spirit of truth have lost their content and are now no more than carcasses. I throw them out, I throw them out . . . My life is not dedicated to the preservation of the dead. I throw out Stephenson's locomotive. But if I throw out the first locomotive, what shall I preserve from all that is not of the present? I will throw out everything because my twenty-four hours must be productive, urgently productive. I will throw out everything from the past except that which is still of service to me. Some things are always of service: art.

* * *

I will always feel certain that man is an active being in a world in action, and not a passive element. The fakir himself confirms it.

An active being carries with him the sense of truth which is his judgement. His judgement is independent and personal, making decisions from one minute to the next. It is an imperative which is at the same time his lucidity and his force. The sense of truth has no formula. You can't get it at the chemist's. This sense of truth is the force of a man. Diogenes replied to Alexander the Great: 'Get out of my light!' The sense of truth has no concern for position or etiquette and does not fear the consequences.

The sun passes once in the twenty-four hours of my day. 'Get out of my light.' I have the right to say that to objects and to ideas, which are no more than lackeys. Each of us is a master: 'Get out of my light.'

Diogenes was a 'cynic'. The word indicates arrogance, but it implies a total, complete commitment. It is this *completeness* which is fine. Arrogance is not at all attractive. Alexander and the barrel of Diogenes are not of our time. Leave arrogance aside.

*_**

When the inexplicable intervenes in man's work, that is to say, when our spirit is projected far from the narrow relation of cause and effect and a feeling of happiness lifts us and carries our thoughts from the brute object to the cosmic phenomenon in time, in space, in the intangible, in all that is visible of the roots spread out around us, nourishing us with the sap of the world – at

Saturn: a true creation.

this point the inexplicable is the miracle of art, the moment when an object, a raw creation, shaped before our eyes, with a form similar for us all, is like a radium, a potential of the mind, a concentrated power, a work of art.

This serves, and will always serve to move us. The mystery is not negligible, is not to be rejected, is not futile. It is the minute of silence in our toil. It awaits the initiate. The initiate is the man of greater strength who will explain . . . one day.

*_**

There is no mystery in the crisis of decorative art; the miracle can occur of an architecture that *will be*, the day when decorative art *ceases to be*.

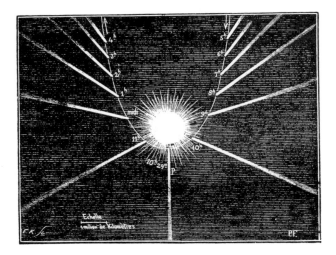

The comet of 1843 . . .

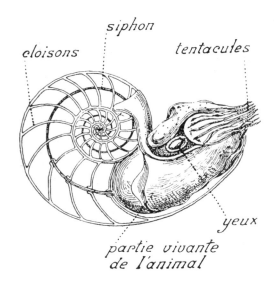

1925

EXPO.
ARTS. DÉCO.

13

We all confront the problem of our surroundings for the sake of our comfort and well-being, for the delight of our hearts, for our pleasure, and also for the satisfaction of a feeling for what is fitting: we would like to be appropriate.

Elimination of the equivocal. Concentration of intention on its proper object. Attention concentrated on the object. An object is required to be made only out of necessity, for a specific purpose, and to be made with perfection. A perfect object is a living organism, animated by the spirit of truth.

Suppose we grant to decorative art the care of our emotional being. Let us accept this proposition. That is, we wish to make ourselves into judges of matters of feeling. It would be a valuable achievement indeed to make each one of us into a prudent judge. In the confusion of our tumultuous times many have become accustomed to think against a background of black. But the tasks of our age, so strenuous, so full of danger, so violent, so victorious, seem to demand of us that we think against a background of white.

Canadian Pacific.

A COAT OF WHITEWASH
THE LAW OF RIPOLIN

If the question of decorative art seems in this year, amid the acclamation of the crowd, the firework displays and the palaces of gilt plaster, to take an important place in our concerns, it is because 1925 is exceptionally the international 'Marathon' of the domestic arts. A tension evident in every country is fostering the illusion of fruitful effort, and adding an extra impetus. The atmosphere is tense. Eloquent showmen have flooded us with 'decorative' schemes and here we are, ready to take our place at the great international presentation of decoration. Behind the decoration we shall find, where expected, the real elements of the tension affecting all countries: the snail is putting together the pieces of his shell, the real question at issue is the house.

Decorative art did not make much impact in the past. But today it is undeniably a live social issue. There is a constant flux and profusion of ideas – signs that a decisive phase is taking shape. Depending on the interpretation to be given to this development, the outlook may be lamentable or encouraging.

At every level of society there is concern for what is a matter of *sentiment*: adorning one's surroundings to make life less empty. Suddenly, after a century of complete indifference, a close, incisive, active concern has gripped everyone. We all confront the problem of our surroundings for the sake of our comfort and well-being, for the delight of our hearts, for our pleasure, and also for the satisfaction of a feeling for what is fitting: we would like to be *appropriate*. It is a remarkable fact that we are in the presence of a *basic* movement, a social movement. I am convinced that in fact what is happening is an architectural movement, a general architectural movement, that is emerging at its due time, when its hour has come – an historic architectural movement. If it is a general architectural movement, then this development is commendable. Architecture is in the smallest things and extends to everything man makes: the apotheosis of the decorative arts in the year 1925 thus marks, admittedly by a paradox, the awakening of the architectural movement of the machine age. There is plenty of tangible evidence: everywhere in every country the daily newspapers, the news magazines, the serious reviews, the 'little reviews', in fact the whole press, have recently added the heading 'Architecture' to their list of contents. Interest extends from the dressmaker's hatbox to the future town-plans of Paris, London or Moscow.

What would be lamentable, in the face of a phenomenon so vast and at the same time touching our hearts so closely as individuals and as a society, would be to see huge amounts of money directed by the State into organising the glorification of the floral hatbox: the building of immense and ostentatious exhibition halls to enshrine in 'sublime' surroundings the escapade of a flower-bud swanning from an umbrella handle to the back of an easy chair.

The Paris Fair, for its part, has turned this unfortunate escapade upside down: in makeshift huts the electricity stands showed us the victory of science, and thereby the inevitable transformation of our social framework. It was an important statement.

At the same time it is true that alongside this grand deployment of human powers which should, it seems, lift us to the new status of demi-gods, we revert, when the work is done, to our emotional base-line. This wild dream into which speculation carries us, is broken off sharp in face of the modest but overriding structure of our emotional being: a human heart which will never change.

Suppose we grant to decorative art the care of this emotional being. With the question thus posed, we cut through the passion-fraught mass of the two opposing causes like a wire through butter, and finally bring order to the contradictory feelings that trouble us.

So we want by means of decorative art to lend our heart a satisfaction worthy of the demi-god who elsewhere constantly imposes on us his violent suggestions. That is, we wish to make ourselves into judges of matters of feeling, and intend to establish a framework within which such matters can find rest.

It would be a valuable achievement indeed to make each one of us a prudent judge. For a long time (even as far back as the first soviets such as M. Léandre Vaillat* in *Temps*), people have been preaching a crusade for art in public places. Confusion. There is art everywhere in the street, which is the museum of the present and the past. All you have to do is to be able to recognise it and it is then superfluous to want to add another art on top of it. Where it is seriously lacking is *in the individual* home. It is there that this absence, multiplied by millions, creates a collective fact with grave social consequences: the forsaking of the home. Art must be brought to the individual and that is why it is useful to give a power of judgement to the individual.

The individual is wanting in judgement.

The new 'Surrealists' (formerly Dadaists) claim to lift themselves above the brute nature of the object and are ready to recognise only relationships which belong to the invisible and subconscious world of the dream. Nevertheless, they compare themselves to radio antennae; thus they raise radio onto their own pedestal, while otherwise pretending to regard it as being of the flattest banality, of the most insignificant 'reality'. And the supremely elegant relationships of their metaphors – as they impress one who is not such a 'high dreamer' – are all the time very clearly dependent on the products of straightforward conscious effort, sustained and logical, cross-checked by the necessary mathematics and geometry – the finality necessary to polished steel, the necessary exactitude for the functioning of mechanisms, etc.

De Chirico writes in the first number of *Revolution Surréaliste* (December 1924): 'They are like levers, as irresistible as those all-powerful machines, those gigantic cranes which raise high over the teeming building-sites sections of floating fortresses with heavy towers like the breasts of antediluvian mammals . . .'

*French writer on regional and cultural matters, born 1878. He published *Le Décor de la vie* in 1920 and 1924 and *Le Rythme de l'architecture* in 1921. J.I.D.

However far you want to carry the exaltation of emotions – even if only to undermine a rationalism which was and is indispensable, and thereby create a new Byronic romanticism – these emotive relationships will continue to be based on *objects*, and the only possible objects are *objects with a function*.

So the poets of Surrealism – a big word that has arrived on the scene during the build-up to the 1925 Exhibition without there being any deliberate connection between them – can only base their poetics on realism, this realism which is the magnificent fruit of the machine age and with which we are still so far from being tired that they themselves hook onto it the skein of their dreams.

The product of the machine age is a realist object capable of high poetry. We approve so much of this object, we are so fond of it, we would so much like to live with it, that our desire adds to its utility the higher dignity of beauty! *The realist object of utility is beautiful.* Such is the final conclusion of the spirit forged in the labours of the age.

So we have to reconsider what is beautiful for us, to recognise what is beautiful for us.

A *beauty* that is made from objects whose relationships exalt us.

* * *

If some Solon imposed these two laws on our enthusiasm:

THE LAW OF RIPOLIN
A COAT OF WHITEWASH

we would perform a moral act: *to love purity*!
we would improve our condition: *to have the power of judgement*!
An act which leads to the joy of life: the pursuit of perfection.

Imagine the results of the Law of Ripolin. Every citizen is required to replace his hangings, his damasks, his wall-papers, his stencils, with a plain coat of white ripolin. *His home* is made clean. There are no more dirty, dark corners. *Everything is shown as it is.* Then comes *inner* cleanness, for the course adopted leads to refusal to allow anything at all which is not correct, authorised, intended, desired, thought-out: no action before thought. When you are surrounded with shadows and dark corners you are at home only as far as the hazy edges of the darkness your eyes cannot penetrate. You are not master in your own house. Once you have put ripolin on your walls you will be *master of yourself*. And you will want to be precise, to be accurate, to think clearly. You will rearrange your house, which your work has disturbed. After your work you will set out what has been produced: you will clear away what cannot be used. You will draw up a new balance sheet, a new sum to be carried forward.

With ripolin you will throw away what has served its purpose and is now scrap. An important act in life; productive morality. You will set on one side what is useful. When we eat, nature knows well how to rid us of what has served its purpose. Without the Law of Ripolin we accumulate, we make our houses into museums or temples filled with votive offerings, turning our mind into a concierge or *custodian*. Moreover we flatter the miser in us and we are gripped and bound by the instinct for material possessions, like Harpagon.* We are led to lying, since we try to camouflage both this ugly accumulation, and our cowardice in not facing a separation. *We set up the cult of the souvenir.* And we lie every day to ourselves. We lie to others. We are false to our destiny, for instead of leaving our mind free to explore the vast continent before us, we confine it in manacles, in the traps, dungeons and ditches of memory.

On white ripolin walls these accretions of dead things from the past would be intolerable: they would leave a mark. Whereas the marks do not show on the medley of our damasks and patterned wall-papers.

If we feel inclined to converse with beings now vanished, is pure memory itself not more lively and accurate than memory roused through the intermediary of dead objects?

The Law of Ripolin would bring the joy of life, the joy of action.

Solon, give us the law of Ripolin.

*
* *

Whitewash exists wherever peoples have preserved intact the balanced structure of a harmonious culture.

Once an extraneous element opposed to the harmony of the system has been introduced, whitewash disappears. Hence the collapse of regional arts – the death of folk culture. Peoples are then obliged to climb by conscious knowledge the long road leading to a new equilibrium.

In the course of my travels I found whitewash wherever the twentieth century had not yet arrived. But all these countries were in the course of acquiring, one after the other, the culture of cities, and the whitewash, which was still traditional, was sure to be driven out in a few years by wall-paper, gilt porcelain, tin 'brassware', cast-iron decoration – driven out by Pathé-Ciné and Pathé-Phono, brutally driven out by industry, which brought complete confusion to their calm souls.

Once factory-made brassware arrives, or porcelain decorated with gilt seashells, whitewash cannot last. It is replaced with wall-paper, which is in the spirit of the new arrivals. Or, as long as whitewash lasts, it means that the brassware has not yet arrived, because the whitewash would show it up. Pathé-Cine or Phono, which are the mark of the times, are not hateful – far

*The miser in Molière's *L'Avare*. J.I.D.

from it – but Pathé incarnates, in these countries living on the morality or centuries of tradition, the dissolving virus which in a matter of years will break everything down. Some time ago, by the 'Sweet Waters of Europe' at the far end of the Golden Horn, I heard the whine of countless gramophones on the caïques plashing the water, and I reckoned that Abdul Hamid was dead, that the Young Turks had arrived, that the Bazaar was changing its signs, and that the West was triumphing. And already today we have Ankara, and the monument to Mustapha-Kemal! Events move fast. The die is cast: one more centuries-old civilisation goes to ruin. No more whitewash in Turkey for a long time to come!

Whitewash has been associated with human habitation since the birth of mankind. Stones are burnt, crushed and thinned with water – and the walls take on the purest white, an extraordinarily beautiful white.

If the house is all white, the outline of things stands out from it without any possibility of mistake; their volume shows clearly; their colour is distinct. The white of whitewash is absolute, everything stands out from it and is recorded absolutely, black on white; it is honest and dependable.

Put on it anything dishonest or in bad taste – it hits you in the eye. It is rather like an X-ray of beauty. It is a court of assize in permanent session. It is the eye of truth.

L'Illustré.   Sultan Mahembe and his two sons.
Three black heads against a white background, fit to govern, to dominate . . . an open door through which
we can see true grandeur.

Studio of M. Ozenfant.

Le Corbusier and Pierre Jeanneret.

Whitewash is extremely moral. Suppose there were a decree requiring all rooms in Paris to be given a coat of whitewash. I maintain that that would be a police task of real stature and a manifestation of high morality, the sign of a great people.

Whitewash is the wealth of the poor and of the rich – of everybody, just as bread, milk and water are the wealth of the slave and of the king.

* *

Law of Ripolin, Coat of Whitewash: elimination of the equivocal. Concentration of intention on its proper object. Attention concentrated on the object. An object is held to be made only out of necessity, for a specific purpose, and to be made with perfection. The perfect object is a living organism, animated by the sense of truth. We have in us an unfailing imperative which is the sense of truth and which recognises in the smoothness of ripolin and the white of whitewash an object of truth. The object of truth radiates power. Between one object of truth and another, astonishing relationships develop. We have the soul of a demiurge, which bases its acts on these objects of truth made by the human genius. The supreme joy, the true joy, is to create: to create objects or hypotheses, but always to respond to this profound primordial function which animates even the lowest cell of organic life: to create.

The machine has inaugurated the age of the demi-gods. Everything has still to be made. Our confident hearts and thrilled eyes are bent unanimously on this future, which is advancing rapidly, bearing us with it.

The time is past when we can be passive beings, adding to the column headed 'Liabilities' our backward-looking thoughts – admissions of defeat, forever-fruitless declarations of love.

Equally the time is past when we – men of vigour in an age of heroic reawakening from the powers of the spirit, in an epoch which rings out with a tragic thunder not far from Doric – can lounge on ottomans and divans among orchids in the scented atmosphere of a seraglio and behave like so many ornamental animals or humming-birds in impeccable evening dress, pinned through the trunk like a collection of butterflies to the swathes of gold, lacquer or brocade on our wall-panelling and hangings.

The Stadium, like the Bank, demands precision and clarity, speed and correctness. Stadium and bank both provide conditions appropriate for action, conditions of clarity like that in a head that has to think. There may be people who think against a background of black. But the tasks of our age – so strenuous, so full of danger, so violent, so victorious – seem to demand of us that we think against a background of white.

CONFESSION

A friend who followed closely the development of the theme in this book as its chapters appeared in *L'Esprit Nouveau*, and who also knew something of my past, said to me: 'You end by denying decorative art. Well, all that is known of you are works of architecture totally denuded of decorative art. People will think: this man has no knowledge of the beauty of the tiny flower and the song of the great Pan which nature trembles to hear. He is fed on theories: his heart is parched: it is easy for him to write off an important cycle of emotions, and the multiplicity of arts which give them expression and perpetuate them. You cannot allow so summary a judgement to be passed on your conclusions, which in fact are the outcome of a long odyssey through the archipelagos of knowledge. You must give a hearing to your moments of doubt and elation during these last twenty-five years – the very period when the form of our age seems to have crystallized in its acceleration towards a profound evolutionary change. You should explain the reason for your idea with an explanation of yourself; at the end of your book you owe your readers the pardonable disclosures of a *confession*.'

Here is that confession.

Twenty-five years ago I took the decision, in that boy's head of mine, that art would be my occupation. If I have today arrived at architecture, it is after having passed through those stages of art where greater liberty seems to prevail, or contact with nature is direct, or the emotions are more immediate. Around 1900 I moved with the heroic-conquering spirit of the time and had assumed that only through the decorative arts would I be engaged in serious work: the 'free arts' seemed to me too devoted to pure pleasure. Renewing the social framework was the talk of the time, while painting was concerned only with sprinkling the sun's rays over the greenery of languid landscapes: few were aware that Cézanne was at work and that Seurat had existed.

My master was an excellent teacher and a real man of the woods, and he made us men of the woods. Nature was the setting where, with my friends, I spent my childhood. Besides, my father was passionately devoted to the mountains and river which made up our landscape. We were constantly on the mountain tops: the vast horizons were familiar. When there was a sea of mist, its infinite expanse was like the real sea – which I had never seen. That was the crowning spectacle. Adolescence is a time of insatiable curiosity. I knew flowers inside-out, the shapes and colours of birds, how a tree grows and how it keeps its balance even in the eye of a storm.

My master had said: 'Only nature can give us inspiration, can be true, can provide a basis for the work of mankind. But don't treat nature like the landscapists who show us only its appearance. Study its causes, forms and vital development, and synthesize them in the creation of *ornaments*.' He had an exalted conception of ornament, which he saw as a kind of microcosm.

For him, there remained three great periods: Egypt with the lotus, Greece with the acanthus, and Gothic with the flowers and beasts of the woods (a radical abridgement of the history of art, you will agree!) Lotus, acanthus, kale or cress. So our task was to study passionately our immediate environment: from the bud to the rhythmic repetition of the hills on the horizon, we would build up the most faithful and moving dictionary of speaking forms. Our style would be a style of the country, a poem to our country. (You see, Monsieur Léandre Vaillat, quite a long time ago I too was a regionalist.)

So that's how it was.

For ten years we composed a kind of ode to our country.

My master had said: 'We are going to renew the house and restore the fine crafts that have disappeared.' There was a score of us choosing our vocation: sculptor in stone, in wood, worker in ceramics or mosaic, glazier, brazier, engraver, etcher, ironworker, jeweller, fresco-painter, etc. What an army! Magnificent enthusiasm and total commitment.

Sundays often found us together at the top of the highest hill. It had pinnacles as well as grandly sweeping slopes: pastures, herds of large cattle, uninterrupted horizons, flights of rooks. We were preparing the future.

'Here,' said the master, 'we will build a monument dedicated to nature and we will make it our lives' purpose. We will leave the town and live under the trees, beside the building which we will gradually fill with our works. It will incorporate the whole landscape – all the fauna and flora. Once a year there will be great festivals held there, with huge braziers lighted at the four corners of the building . . .'

During these years art-workshops had been established. We had decorated chapels and concert halls, made furniture and jewellery, and put tombs in the cemetery. Most of us had left our family homes and rented barns outside the town to which we returned in the evenings to be closer to nature. It was REAL LIFE. Big words: life! Exaltation amid the anguish of those young hearts of ours. Too much energy was pouring out, and the close-knit organisation of bourgeois society constrained us to continence in everything. Young people are too *true*: they cause disruption: they are excluded from the impervious enclosure within which a bourgeois society huddles. We had founded a school (a little like the Bauhaus of Weimar ten years later). The teachers of the schools of the town had then begun secretly nibbling away. Rivalries, calumnies, lies and spite . . . From time to time even now I meet by chance in the street people who were my pupils. It was a bitter struggle against the sceptical public and against the rival school. Finally the socialists were our undoing. Why the socialists? That was perhaps my first shock as an adult.

First one of us, then another left to travel. And returned. And was astonished and concerned to see the excitement and faith which still inspired those who had stayed behind. One day I picked my way under the vaulted ceiling of a hall which my companions were decorating, and spoke in a heretical vein. 'Off to sea with you!' they shouted at me from the scaffolding.

. . . .

The crunch came one day.

After fifteen years it was all over. Dispersal, bitterness, jealousies, hatreds.

The master had forgotten that in him as in us there were fiercely obstinate, egotistical hearts. The romantic, dazzling adventure was over.

The bourgeois of the town were reassured: the last ripples were quieted on the waters that had been so violently disturbed: the game of cards could be calmly resumed and the cigars puffed.

Here ends my first chapter.

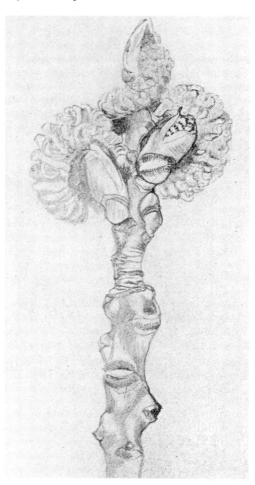

* * *

I then explored the big cities one after the other, to learn, to live, to look for where to apply energies eager to produce, and I tasted their brutality. Big cities are deserts for the young where one starves before a thousand closed doors behind which one can make out the clicking of forks.

The life of a lost dog.

The schools of the big cities! Adolescent boys and girls: the men with long hair, the women with short hair. Bohemianism still existed in those days, long before the war.

'I am a kid looking for . . . a teacher!' Six years here, four years there. The instruction seemed slow and sullen, as unapproachable as a curled-up hedgehog. Should one imprison oneself in one of those galleys, in Paris, Vienna, Munich, Berlin, when one felt life bubbling outside – a life different from the one spoken of in the schools?

A search for truth in libraries. Books. The books are endless – where to begin? Suddenly one falls into a hole. It is dark and one can no longer make sense of anything.

From the museums I acquired certainties without holes, without snares. The works there are like integral numbers, and the conversation is without

Romanesque.

Assyria.

pretence: intimacy is at the discretion of the questioner – the work always
answers the questions put. Works in museums are good schools.

The museums are large; I put my questions only to what is not called
Great Art. Of course I went on Sundays to see the Cimabues, the Breughels,
the Raphaels, the Tintorettos, etc. But to work, to draw, to understand the
full richness that one must give one's work, and the degree of concentration,
of transposition, of invention, of re-creation that is required, I settled where
no one at that time put his easel – far from the *Grande Galerie*. I was always
alone . . . with the attendants.

At the Musée Cluny, for the tapestries, miniatures, Persian plates.

At the Guimet, for all the deities in bronze, wood or stone.

At the gallery of M. Pottier, for the Etruscans and Greeks.

At the Trocadero, for the portals of the French cathedrals.

At the Pavillon de Marsan for Persian carpets and brocades.

At the Museum (of Natural History) to learn many lessons. There is
much at this museum to analyse: shells, birds, big pre-historic skeletons and
skeletons of all present day animals. First introduction to the mechanism of
things.

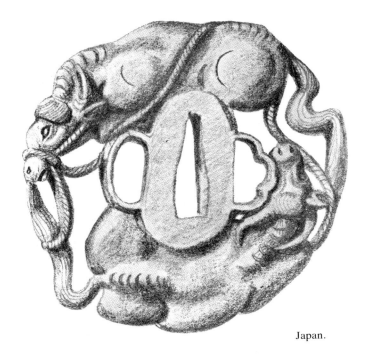

Japan.

In the Ethnographic Museum at the Trocadero: the Mexicans, the Peruvians, the Negroes. One was alone there in 1907! Not a cat! The negroes – what a revelation! Nimba, god of maternity.

At the ethnographic Museum of Berlin, the same.

Middle Ages.

Egypt.

In London, the South Kensington Museum and the dazzling Hindu dancing girls.

At the British Museum, the art of Benin.

The popular arts, pots and carpets at the ethnographic Museum of Belgrade.

The Etruscans in the ethnographic Museum of Florence.

Antique decorative art in the Museum of Naples, and at Pompeii.

What lessons, what lessons! What drawings, conscientiously putting and then answering questions with the precise outline of an eloquent form!

* * *

In 1907 I had knocked on the door of M. Grasset, who advised me to go to see Auguste Perret.

Auguste Perret had just completed the Ponthieu garage and his apartment building on the Rue Franklin. He used to say to anyone who would listen, with the sound of battle in his voice: 'I do reinforced concrete.' And yes, it was a question of doing battle in those days. It was a heroic hour

Peru.

and Auguste Perret was the man of the hour. He has a clear place which will always be his as years go by.

Auguste Perret was astonished to find me so fond of museums. 'I would study mathematics if I had the time', he said. 'They form the character.'

Romanesque.

Greek.

I studied mathematics and in practice they were never of any use to me afterwards. But they may have formed my character.

Auguste Perret also said: 'One must build with perfection: decoration generally hides a want of perfection.'

Chaldea.

Negro.

I was very keen on construction. I spent whole afternoons on Notre-Dame, equipped with an enormous set of keys from the Ministry of Fine Arts. I got to know the tiniest recesses of the cathedral, right to the tips of the

Crete.

Greek.

towers, pinnacles and flying buttresses. For me, it was the Gothic epic poem. But the admiration which I would gladly have expressed for its Gothic form and poetry was withdrawn when it came to the construction. Today I am enraptured by the primordial beauty of a cathedral's plan, and stupefied by

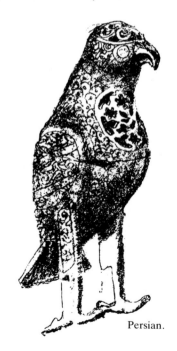

Persian.

the primordial plastic poverty of the work itself. The Gothic plan and shape are magnificent, sparkling with ingenuity. But the promise is not fulfilled in the test of our eyes. An astonishing climax of achievement for the engineer, with plastic failure.

* *
*

By a chance set of circumstances I came to spend more than a year travelling in Germany. I was commissioned to study the organisation of the decorative arts in Germany. I had introductions which opened the doors of factories, offices, schools, design studios. I visited everything, put questions about everything. I saw all that Germany had set on foot: an extraordinary organisation, a huge output. The Director of the decorative arts organisation in Bavaria said to me: 'I have been round our factories and told their directors – if you don't alter your methods of production without delay and apply to the letter the designs of our decorative artists I will mount the power of this organisation against you and you will be wiped out! And the industrialists took their cue one after the other.'

I was naturally impressed, but this terrible doubt then crept in: so what? Can decorative artists with sketches made on paper at the call of fancy, modify the inexorable, almost automatic exigencies of industrial technology? Can the industrial product be improved or revolutionised by quite extraneous intervention? Does the existence of the decorative artist whom I then admired, rest on this inordinate claim?

In some workshops for the fabrication of metalwork and art-ironwork I saw an atrocious machine in action – a hammering machine. It received smooth and perfect iron sections and in a few moments made them all pitted, like scrap-iron.

That was at the time of the great crusade for the hand-made.

Stage One: man, without other equipment, shapes the iron ingot with hammer-blows as best he can: he does not manage to make something that meets his aspirations. But what an effort all the same, what striving for perfection!

Stage Two: the machine, now that it has been invented, draws out the steel in pure, smooth and mathematically exact shapes. The age of steel replaces the iron age. Incalculable consequences.

Stage Three: the decorative artist. Religion: the hand-made. Conscientiously he invents the pitting machine and makes *by machine* objects with the look of the hand-made. What an atrocity!

My doubt grew deeper and deeper, and fifteen years later I am of the clear opinion that industry by itself is following the course of its own evolution. The designer–decorator is the enemy, the parasite, the false brother.

Istanbul.

(My report on the teaching of design, dated 1914, called for the closing of the schools of decorative art.)

* * *

This third chapter again finds me travelling abroad in quest of the lesson that will clarify my mind, and in an attempt to capture the source of art, the reason for art, the role of art. I acquainted myself with the fashions of Paris, Vienna, Berlin, Munich. Everything about all these fashions seemed to be dubious: but I knew that reinforced concrete and iron would generate their own form which would be quite new. I was impressed with the arbitrariness of the creations of that time. I embarked on a great journey, which was to be decisive, through the countryside and cities of countries still considered unspoilt. From Prague I went down the Danube, I saw the Serbian Balkans, then Rumania, then the Bulgarian Balkans, Adrianople, the Sea of Marmora, Istanbul (and Byzantium), Bursa in Asia.

Then Athos.

Then Greece.

Then the south of Italy and Pompeii.

Rome.

I saw the grand and eternal monuments, glories of the human spirit.

Istanbul.

Above all, I succumbed to the irresistible attraction of the Mediterranean. And it was high time, after ten years' work (published in all the reviews) on German decorative art and architecture.

The Turkey of Adrianople, Byzantium, of Santa Sophia or Salonica, the Persia of Bursa, the Parthenon, Pompeii, then the Coliseum. Architecture was revealed to me. Architecture is the magnificent play of forms under light. Architecture is a coherent construct of the mind. Architecture has nothing to do with decoration. Architecture is in the great buildings, the difficult and high-flown works bequeathed by time, but *it is also in the smallest hovel*, in an enclosure-wall, in everything, sublime or modest, which contains sufficient geometry to establish a mathematical relationship.

After such a voyage my respect for decoration was finally shattered. I have seen the countries famous for their regional styles, so grotesquely evoked on the stage of the Opéra-Comique. There is no decoration which can summon up the feelings of a traveller: there is architecture, which is pure, unified, form – structure and modelling – and there are works of art: Phidias or the pot of the potter in the Serbian Balkans. An emotional response is provoked by a complex of forms assembled in a precise relationship: horizontals and verticals. Or else it is the work which by the progressive distillation of folk cultures reveals to us a type-thought, potentially universal, the language of the heart of mankind. The folk cultures showed

Danube.

me how serious is every lasting act, how conditioned, how much a development of previous acts like itself: how the individual is absorbed in the community, how the community gives its sap to the individual under the
influence of an outstanding spirit and a powerful mind. There is never a
diversion, an oddity, a 'bit of a lark'. There is the desire to make a beautiful
poem or a good tool. In both cases all one's art and one's artlessness are
called for. Our own day, with its youngsters with their cars and their 'chicks'

Al-Meidan.

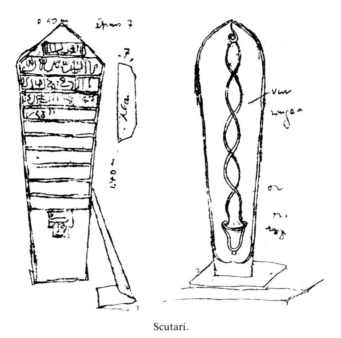

Scutari.

to practice simplicity? The simplicity of the folk cultures is the sum of the achievements of centuries.

Istanbul.

Eyoub.

This long voyage lasted nearly a year. As a free pilgrim, with my bag on my back, guided by spur-of-the-moment impulses, I crossed countries on foot, on horseback, by boat or motorcar, coming up against the basic unity of the fundamental human elements amid the diversity of races. At its end, I had become convinced that a new century had arrived – the twentieth, that the achievements of the past were complete, and that a continuous and irreversible forward movement grips one epoch after another, and in due course leads the peoples of the world on to the next stage.

Santa Sophia.

'. . . The judgement of the public is confused. Bric-à-brac and all that is pretentious, unseemly and horrible is paraded. Complete ignorance. We ourselves carry the deadly germ that goes around in the unspoilt countries, ruining the hearts that used to be simple and believing, and the arts that used

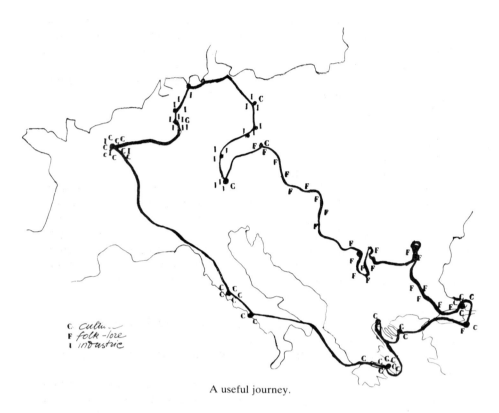

C. *culture*
F *folk-lore*
I *industrie*

A useful journey.

Byzantium. The Aqueduct of Valens.

to be normal, healthy and natural. And I feel that it is a question not of reacting but of acting. For a cleaning out is a vital necessity, and since people have no wish to perish, they will return, yes, to health and thereby to beauty, out of simple desire to live. They are returning all over the world: scales are falling from their eyes. The cancerous germ is coming up against the fine young vigorous germ, born from do-or-die. There is no desire to die . . .' (Travel notebook, 1911).

Return.

Digestion.

One conviction: we must begin again from scratch.

We must set out the problem.

The whirlpool of life. It is not a question of aesthetics. Between the ages of twenty and thirty – that's when one rounds the Cape of Storms. That's when a being's deepest drives are active and a life finds its course. The choice of one's life is made without one being aware of it, without one being able to make any pretence. This way or that. There is a bar deep within us which hardens, takes shape and is aligned in a certain direction. At thirty, one is in a definite place, having or not having passed the Cape of Storms.

. . . .

A morass.

I found myself in industry. A factory. Machines. Taylorism, cost prices, maturities, balance-sheets. That was all it was.

Directing a technical consultancy: it was after the war; everywhere dreams of organisation, of creation.

To conceive, create and organise an enterprise, an individual productive unit: in fact a kind of living thing . . . which can also die! A tough job at a time of economic crises, statistical curves going mad. It is fine for the mind to be ruled by an ardent discipline. Effervescent dreams, icy reason: with the keel gyrating wildly, one must hold onto the helm.

Cold reason.

Exercise of the will.

Formulation of a clear, detached judgement.

Oh, the Bohemia of the Boul'Mich! One does not run onto the field for a tough match dressed as a Bohemian. It was during those long serious years that I attuned myself to the diapason. The diapason is the very *raison d'être* of a society at work. The how and why of the social phenomenon. Once one has got away from the academies of design and opened one's eyes to the social complex, one learns to consult the diapason every day, to adjust one's nascent dream to the countless elements which must ultimately accept its products as useful. Attuned to the diapason, the artist has a *destination* for the product of his work.

***

I met Ozenfant in 1918. A clear mind. The country was reviving: it was our definite opinion that an age of steel was beginning. A period of construction was going to follow the anxieties, disorganisation and experiments of the past.

In 1920, together with Paul Dermée, we launched L'ESPRIT NOUVEAU, *An International Review of Contemporary Activity*. We wanted to construct without further hesitation, to add every day one new certainty yielded by analysis, a certainty in a cycle which will go on being born and developing – and dying, as we are well aware. But we are in the upward stage of the cycle, striving to reach the solider ground close to the central axis of its movement. We said: there exists a new spirit, a spirit of construction and synthesis guided by a clear conception. There are pretty flowers to be picked along the side of the path, away from the paths, the beaten paths. To make a bouquet of them is an alluring temptation – to amuse oneself, amuse oneself madly. The age lends itself marvellously to cock-and-bull stories. Just think: there is plenty to play with. Generations are taken up with this great event; a faith prevails, a total disinterestedness, a passion for conquest, a superb drive which thrusts this epoch forward in quest of victories . . . And there is still M. Homais, of the Second Empire, and the generation of our fathers who protest, resist, refuse, mock, laugh, insult, deny. We are poor and we run round the race-track, exhausted and emotional. Our fathers sit in the stands, and in their midst the tricolour sash of M. Fallières* still seems visible. Our fathers are smoking fat cigars and wearing top hats. They are fine, our fathers, and we are what we are – thin as street cats. That is what provokes the grimace of the embittered, the cock-and-bull stories of the fanciful, and the alienation of the youngest who have not yet set their hands to work.

We have refused to pick flowers off the beaten track. We have tried, with our minds open and our hearts not stoppered in scent bottles, to grasp what really is happening and help give expression to its direction.

---

*Presumably Armand-Clément Fallières, President of France 1906–13. J.D.